The Online Rules of Successful Companies is chock-full
of real-world examples and solid, commonsense ideas for
embracing the Internet and putting it to work for you. the
goal here isn't to help you position yourself for the red-hot
initial public offering. The goal is to help you use the
Internet to build a solid, sustainable, and profitable
business.

Rich Jaroslovsky
Founding President, Online News Association
Former Managing Editor, *The Wall Street Journal Online*

Imagine having one of the most successful and practical
(in the classic sense) people to have worked in Internet-
based businesses telling you how it's done and illustrating
each point with vivid examples of companies and practices
that are still making money. Robin Miller is the person and
this is the book. Accept no other.

Paul Jones
University of North Carolina, Chapel Hill
Director of ibiblio.org

the online rules of
Successful
Companies
The Fool-Proof Guide to Building Profits

ISBN 0-13-066842-7

FT Prentice Hall
FINANCIAL TIMES

In an increasingly competitive world, it is quality
of thinking that gives an edge. an idea that opens new
doors, a technique that solves a problem, or an insight
that simply helps make sense of it all.

We must work with leading authors in the fields of
management and finance to bring cutting-edge thinking
and best learning practice to a global market.

Under a range of leading imprints, including
Financial Times Prentice Hall, we create world-class
print publications and electronic products giving readers
knowledge and understanding which can then be
applied, whether studying or at work.

To find out more about our business and professional
products, you can visit us at www.phptr.com

the online rules of

Successful Companies

The Fool-Proof Guide to Building Profits

buildprofitsonline.com

Robin "Roblimo" Miller

FT Prentice Hall
FINANCIAL TIMES

An imprint of PEARSON Education
London • New York • San Francisco • Toronto • Sydney
Tokyo • Singapore • Hang Kong • Cape Town • Madrid •
Paris • Milan • Munich • Amsterdam

Library of Congress Cataloging-in-Publication Data

Miller, Robin, 1952-
   The online rules of successful companies : the fool-proof guide to builing profits /
Robin Miller.
      p. cm. -- (Financial Times Prentice Hall)
   Includes index.
   ISBN 0-13-066842-7
   1. Electronic commerce--Management. 2. Internet industry--Management. I. Title. II.
Financial Times Prentice Hall books.

HF5548.32 .M54 2002
658.8'4--dc21   2002075287

Editorial/production supervision: *Laura Burgess*
Cover design director: *Jerry Votta*
Cover design: *Nina Scuderi*
Art director: *Gail Cocker-Bogusz*
Interior design: *Maureen Eide*
Manufacturing manager: *Alexis R. Heydt-Long*
V.P., Executive editor: *Tim Moore*
Editorial assistant: Allyson Kloss
Development editor: *Russ Hall*
Marketing manager: *Bryan Gambrel*

© 2003 Pearson Education, Inc.
Publishing as Financial Times Prentice Hall
Upper Saddle River, New Jersey 07458

Financial Times Prentice Hall books are widely used by corporations and government agencies
for training, marketing, and resale.

For information regarding corporate and government bulk discounts please contact:
                  Corporate and Government Sales
                  (800) 382-3419 or
                  corpsales@pearsontechgroup.com

Slashdot, freshmeat, Linux.com, NewsForge, and OSDN are all trademarks or registered trademarks of
VA Software, Inc.; Linux is a registered trademark owned by Linus Torvalds; Wired News is a
registered trademark of Terra Lycos; NewsFactor and NewsFactor Network are trademarks of Triad
Commerce Group, LLC; Opera Browser is a registered trademark of Opera Software; Microsoft
Internet Explorer, FrontPage, and Windows are registered trademarks of Microsoft Corporation; AOL,
Netscape, and Mozilla are registered trademarks of AOL Time Warner. All other company and product
names mentioned herein are the trademarks or registered trademarks of their respective owners.

ISBN: 0-13-066842-7

Pearson Education LTD
Pearson Education Australia PTY, Limited
Pearson Education Singapore, Pte. Ltd.
Pearson Education North Asia Ltd.
Pearson Education Canada, Ltd.
Pearson Educacion de Mexico, S.A. de C.V.
Pearson Education—Japan
Pearson Education Malaysia, Pte. Ltd.

FINANCIAL TIMES PRENTICE HALL BOOKS

For more information, please go to www.ft-ph.com

*This book is dedicated to
my wife
and to my OSDN coworkers
who have all been so supportive*

Contents

Resources   173

Index   177

Foreword

It is hardly original to observe that the popular view of the Internet has changed radically in its short lifetime. In the space of well under a decade, those perceptions have progressed from playground for geeks and scientists to curiosity to phenomenon to burst bubble. Yet to dismiss the importance of the Internet to companies today because of the failure of so many ill-conceived business plans is to miss the online medium's real and continuing impact.

Many transforming technologies have gone through the same evolution that the Net has—so many, in fact, that it seems a massive shakeout is not just characteristic but is almost a requirement somewhere along the way. The automobile, for one, followed much the same pattern in its early life; names such as Doble and Stutz were the Kozmo and Pets.com of their day. Yet for all the car companies that failed and money that was lost, no one today seriously argues the point that the automobile profoundly reshaped our lives. So it is with the Internet.

With the clarity of 20/20 hindsight, we can now see that the Net didn't force successful, established companies out of business, to be replaced by legions of unproven upstarts. Instead, its real impact can be seen in how many of those successful, established companies have embraced it to extend their reach, better serve their current customers, and entice new ones. We are no longer quite so starry-eyed about the Net, but we can see things more clearly now. And what's clearest is that the Net has in a few short years become integral to the way companies do business in the 21st century.

Along the way, we have relearned some old lessons and learned some new ones. The most important lesson may be that the same things that make companies successful in the offline world—the same standards, values, and commitment to the customer—can make them successful online. The Internet, as all of us have conclusively seen (and some of us have conclusively demonstrated), won't turn bad ideas into brilliant ones or lousy companies into winners. But, intelligently utilized, it can make good ideas and companies better.

And that's where this book comes in. *The Online Rules of Successful Companies: The Fool-Proof Guide to Building Profits* is chock full of real-world examples and solid, common sense ideas for embracing the Internet and putting it to work for you. The goal here isn't to help you position yourself for that red-hot initial public offering. The goal is to help you use the Internet to build a solid, sustainable, and profitable business.

Along the way, you'll get plainspoken advice about designing a successful Web site; about the strengths and weaknesses of selling goods online; about how to get noticed; about how to use the Net to hold down costs; and about how to use other, non-Web services of the Net (e.g., live chat, email) to establish a bond with your customers or audience.

We who were involved in the early days of the Web explosion have known for a long time that if you look up the word "iconoclast" in the dictionary, you'll find a picture of Robin Miller. *The Online Rules of Successful Companies* doesn't disappoint on that score; it delights in puncturing the myths and pretensions of the medium and many of its champions. But its iconoclasm is matched by its down-to-earth advice and wealth of specific, vivid examples. Provocative and practical, it deserves to be read, studied, and followed not only by every Internet entrepreneur, but by every entrepreneur of any stripe interested in doing business in the Information Age.

Rich Jaroslovsky
Founding President, Online News Association
Former Managing Editor, *The Wall Street Journal Online*
Short Hills, New Jersey
July, 2002

Introduction

The basic thesis of this book is very simple and old-fashioned: that the best—indeed, the only—way to make money on the Internet is to take in more than you spend.

For some reason, between the time the Internet first opened up to commercial activity in 1994 and the end of the 20th century, thousands of so-called visionaries decided this hoary business rule didn't apply online. An awful lot of supposedly hard-headed investors and entrepreneurs bought into this delusion and paid dearly for their insanity. Billions of dollars were poured into dubious schemes. Sound management practices were ignored. Money was thrown around as if there was an endless stream of it cascading down, like rain in a thunderstorm, on Silicon Valley, Silicon Alley, Silicon Prairie, Silicon Harbor, Silicon Swamp, Silicon Coast, Silicon Whatever. All over the world, city fathers and mothers decided that getting "Silicon" into a place name guaranteed endless investments and high-paying jobs; that everyone touched by the Internet was going to be so rich that they wouldn't notice a few dollars one way or the other if bonds were floated and taxes were raised to pay for the infrastructure needed to turn this place or that place into an Internet Mecca full of high-rent lofts and offices all tied together by millions of strands of fiberoptic cable.

Even at the height of this madness a few of us wondered how long the investor-driven money shower would last, and prepared for the day when, inevitably, it would end. We were laughed at for our conservative business plans and cost-cutting—even stingy— management methods, but we are the ones who still have Internet jobs and businesses and will probably have them for the rest of our working lives, while the high-rollers who thought we were silly a few years ago are now sending us their resumes.

Every Game Has Rules

The practices and tactics I advocate in *The Online Rules of Successful Companies* certainly can't guarantee success, but if you apply them correctly you will have a much better chance of making money on the Internet than you'll have if you don't follow them. Most of the basic "rules" in this book apply to any size company, anywhere in the world, whether the Internet itself is its central profit focus or it is a business that operated successfully for decades or even centuries before the word "online" became part of our vocabularies.

It doesn't matter whether you are an individual entrepreneur working from home or an executive for a multi-national corporation; it is as easy for a large company to put up a bad site as it is for a small company to put up a good one. Any size business can overspend on its Internet presence or have unrealistic expectations for it, and any size business can use the Internet as a tool to reach more customers, at lower cost, than it can reach through any other communications medium ever developed—if it uses the Internet correctly.

I have worked hard to avoid programming jargon in this book. It is about the business of the Internet, not its technical aspects. I mention terms like "bandwidth" and "information layering" when they are appropriate, but their meanings should be obvious from context for almost anyone who has ever browsed a Web site or sent and received email.

On the other side of the coin, programmers and Web developers who don't have a lot of business knowledge shouldn't be intimidated by this book, either. Most of the business advice in *The Online Rules of Successful Companies* is nothing but old-fashioned common sense applied to a new medium, and shouldn't be hard to understand—even though a lot of people seem to have trouble realizing that business on the Internet is still business, that advertising on the Internet is still advertising, and that the basic rules of customer service apply online the same way they apply in a "brick-and-mortar" store where clerks wait on customers in person.

Learn From the Past

When the Internet was a brand-new business tool, we were all experimenting, trying to figure out how to use it. Everyone made plenty of mistakes. I made my share, and I freely admit it.

Things are different now. We have had time to watch some Internet businesses succeed and others fail. We have a pretty good idea of what makes one site easy to use and another one hard to navigate. We are all still experimenting and learning—and making mistakes—but we are no longer blindly trying to make money online without any real idea of how to do it. We no longer need to grope in the dark.

That is the point of this book: that we finally have enough Internet business history, positive and negative, behind us that if we study that history and let it guide us, instead of praying that the Internet Fairy will touch us with her Magic Money Wand, we can sit down and consciously, rationally build profits online by emulating the best habits and behaviors of effective Internet companies, while avoiding the mistakes made by the many ineffective ones that started back in the 20th century and didn't make it into the 21st.

CHAPTER ONE

What Makes the Internet So Powerful?

The Internet is the lowest cost system ever developed to communicate with a potential audience of hundreds of millions of people all over the world. Even locally, the cost of a simple Web site is usually less than the cost of a modest ad in a business telephone directory. A Web site can also give more information than a telephone directory ad, including color photos, detailed descriptions of products and services, and price information that can be changed at any moment, for any reason, instead of waiting for a printed directory's next publication cycle.

As a news medium, the Internet is faster and more flexible than a newspaper or magazine. A story can be added to a Web site instantly at any time of the day or night. There are no deadlines (except self-imposed ones) for Internet news. The "printing press" is always on, you might say. Even television news, aside from a few 24-hour news channels, must usually wait for scheduled news broadcast times instead of breaking into entertainment programming whenever a new story comes along. Television is also constrained by its necessarily linear information delivery format. It must tell a story, then another story, then take a break for advertising, then tell another story, and so on, in sequence. A viewer cannot choose to view only a few stories that he or she finds interesting, which may occupy only five minutes out of a 30-minute newscast. On the Internet, a reader is free not only to choose to view just those stories in which he or she is most interested, but also gets to choose the order in which he or she sees them. If sports scores are the highest item on today's agenda, **click** and there's the sports section, as easy as turning a newspaper page. Another **click** and there's the score from the game that just ended, possibly with video highlights only one more **click** away.

Corrections, changes, and updates to a story published on the Internet can be made as fast as they come in without waiting for a printing press to roll. Breaking news alerts can be sent instantly by email to subscribers who request this service, and a reader can instantly communicate with an online publication's editors via email or, if the publication has this facility, post his or her comments on a "message board" for other readers to see right away, without waiting for a fax or mail to get through and an editor to look the message over and perhaps include it in the "letters to the editor" section several days after the original story ran.

An online publication can also offer an advertiser something that is not available in any other medium: ads that link directly, with one **click**, to a Web page full of compelling reasons to buy the advertised product or service. Even if only a fraction of one percent of all people who see a Web ad **click** on it, that is still an infinitely higher percentage than can click on a magazine ad or TV spot for additional information—or even to buy a product directly from the advertiser right now. Even if few readers **click** on an individual online ad and buy right now, a Web ad still has the same branding and general "get the name out" effect as advertising in other media. If the cost of an online ad is similar to the cost of one in another medium, it represents a better value because of the ability it gives an advertiser to give an interested person an entire Web site full of information right away, only one **click** removed from the online publication in which that ad is running.

But the most direct way to make money online, no matter how a merchant gets traffic to his or her Web site, is to sell over the Internet. Ecommerce has had its ups and downs, but the overall trend is upward, and it is likely to stay that way for many years to come. Putting up a "catalog" Web site is far less expensive than printing and mailing paper catalogs, and the Web site can have "instant" ordering and credit card acceptance built right into it, whereas a paper catalog can generate only phone orders that require a horde of (expensive) live operators to process or mail-in order forms that a customer must fill out, fold, place in an envelope, and mail instead of going **click** right now and spending a few seconds typing in an address and credit card information, then going **click** once again to buy, right now, without having to look for a stamp.

An online catalog, just like an online news source, has the advantage over its paper counterpart of instant update capability. If a supplier's price changes, the price to customers can change nearly immediately. A blurb for an overstocked item can be placed on a Web site's front page to boost sales today, and email can alert valued customers to special values or sales faster and cheaper than postal mail or any kind of mass media advertising.

Even a business that doesn't sell directly online can use the Internet as an advertising medium. A restaurant, for example, can post its entire menu on its Web site, right down to daily specials, at less cost than any other method of putting detailed information about the establishment into prospective customers' hands. A local business such as a restaurant may be "wasting" the international potential of the Internet; there may be only a few thousand Internet users within a reasonable distance of that establishment. But that localization factor doesn't really matter. If a reasonable percentage of nearby Internet users see the restaurant's site and come in to eat, the site will more than pay for itself. As a bonus for a local business, a Web site will draw trade from out-of-towners because of its international reach. Consider this scenario: You are in Seoul, Korea, and you're traveling to Charlottesville, Virginia, USA. You need to find a hotel and places to eat. You almost certainly don't have a Charlottesville telephone directory handy, but if you have an Internet connection, it takes only a few minutes to use a search engine such as Google (*www.google.com/*) to find a restaurant that suits your taste, either directly through Google or through one of the many localized directories that will show up on your screen if you use the words "Restaurant" and "Charlottesville" as your key search words. So, hypothetical traveler from Korea, you have found a place to eat in Charlottesville, and probably a place to stay and even a nearby store or two, all through the Internet. From a merchant's point of view, you represent a business which he or she would never have gotten without the Internet (and a well-designed Web site). The question for even the smallest local business owner isn't, "Can I afford a Web site?" but, "How can I make an effective Web site without spending too much money?"

Actually, companies of all sizes should be asking themselves, "How can I make the most effective use of the Internet without spending too much money?"

Let's start answering that question by focusing on what the Internet *can* and *cannot* do for your business.

There are only three kinds of commercial Internet activity. That's all. Three. You can use the Internet to provide news or information, to sell goods or services directly online, or as a promotional device for an offline business. You can't use the Internet to ship physical goods, cook food, or build a house, but you can certainly use it as an advertising medium, and possibly as a direct sales channel, for a business that does one of these things. You could use a Web site designed to promote the sale of new homes to provide news about the neighborhood where the development is located, and many Web sites that are promotional brochures at heart do this sort of thing, but I don't believe this is a good idea. Trying to make a Web page or any other advertising message too broad takes away from its focus and detracts from its main message. It is almost always better to do one thing well than to try to do many things and do all of them poorly.

Examples of Successful, Tightly Focused Web Sites

Selling Mexican Food Online: *MexGrocer.com*

MexGrocer.com is an online extension of the U.S. Division of *HERDEZ*, one of Mexico's leading wholesale grocery distributors. The site doesn't have any news or information on it that doesn't directly describe products it sells except for recipes that use products it sells and occasional bits of information about restaurants that buy wholesale from *MexGrocer.com* (see Figure 1–1). Every page, and almost every word on every page, is devoted to selling Mexican food products either directly or indirectly.

MexGrocer.com is a sterling example of a site that sells effectively, with just enough non-sales information mixed in to make it worth a few moments' reading time even if you aren't interested in buying any Mexican food products today. Perhaps you'll bookmark

■ Figure 1–1   _MexGrocer.com_ home page.

it and come back to buy something another time. If you enjoy Mexican food, chances are that you will become a _MexGrocer.com_ customer sooner or later.

Delivering Information Online: Wired News

Wired News (_www.wired.com_) is at the opposite end of the spectrum from _MexGrocer.com_. It's a pure news site, supported entirely by advertising.

Wired News makes no direct attempt to sell anything to its readers. All it sells are ads to advertisers. Friends who work for _Wired News_ say it is consistently profitable. It has a small staff and a large readership, and these two factors are the keys to running a profitable ad-supported news or information Web site.

The fact that _Wired News_ is not tied directly to anyone who manufactures or sells anything is a big point in its favor, and helps it to gain and keep its readers' trust. News sites tied closely to manufacturers, and news sections on ecommerce sites, are inherently suspect. If General Motors owned _Road & Track_ magazine, nobody would be surprised if the Corvette was always the top-rated sports car, but no one would believe _Road & Track_ ratings, either.

MSNBC (*www.msnbc.com*) is partly owned by Microsoft. *Slate* (*www.slate.com*), the online magazine, is a purely Microsoft-owned property. They both suffer from the perception that they are always going to go a little easy on Bill Gates and may be a tad harder on Windows competition (such as the Linux operating system) than other news outlets. Even though I personally believe Microsoft has done a good job of leaving both *MSNBC* and *Slate* alone to report the news without any corporate interference, there is always going to be doubt in their online audience members' minds about how fairly *MSNBC* and *Slate* treat news about Microsoft.

News published directly on a corporate, sales-oriented Web site is even more suspect. There is nothing wrong with publishing news about the company itself or any new products or services it is offering, but would you believe "news" about warehouse operations and material handling published on a forklift manufacturer's Web site? Probably not. If it had taken the same space and devoted it directly to selling forklifts, it would have more credibility—and would probably sell more forklifts.

The beauty of the Internet, in many eyes, is that almost anything can be published freely on it without interference from editors or restrictive governments. For people using the Internet for legitimate business purposes, this freedom means that their online message may be taken with more skepticism than it would be if it were delivered to consumers in a newspaper or on television, which is not a good thing. When a character named Alex Chiu (*www.alexchiu.com*) touts "immortality devices" on his Web site, and even achieves a certain measure of online notoriety by doing so even though there is no medical evidence that his devices work, a company selling legitimate, medically-approved health aids through a Web site that may show up in search engine listings near or even next to Chiu's must be extra-conscious of public perception, and extra-careful to be so truthful that no sensible person confuses its product claims with those made by hucksters like Chiu.

Perhaps all the material handling industry news on our hypothetical forklift company's site is entirely honest, but the perception problem is still there. In general, it is best to avoid any action online that might cause your credibility to be questioned, including trying to mix news and sales too closely together. It's better to stick to one or the other instead of trying to do both.

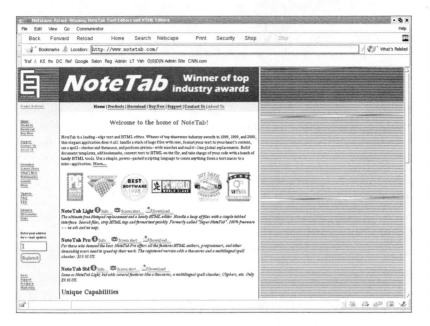

Figure 1–2 The *NoteTab* main page is no thing of beauty, but it delivers a powerful sales message.

Pure Ecommerce: NoteTab

Eric Fookes of Geneva, Switzerland, has been selling a piece of software called *NoteTab* online since 1995. NoteTab is commonly recognized as one of the finest (and least expensive) Windows HTML and text editors around. It is available only as a download through *www.notetab.com*. Fookes Software is privately held, quite small, and consistently profitable. Besides *NoteTab*, it sells several other programs and a few screensaver photo galleries, but *NoteTab* is the company's star offering. This is an extremely focused company, and its *NoteTab* Web site reflects this focus (see Figure 1–2). The only news it carries is about new or updated Fookes Software products. From beginning to end, this site is about selling *NoteTab*, and it does its job very, very well.

No one would call this site great art. But does it need to be anything other than what it is? It has all the basics in place. It's well-placed in most search engines, and the *NoteTab* program is listed prominently in all popular Windows software and shareware directories, which makes it even easier to find than if it were listed only in search engines. As far as I know, Fookes has never run a paid ad or solicited venture capital. He wrote a good piece of software, and he has kept updating it and adding useful features since day one. He gives away a "Light" version of *NoteTab* for free, and sells the "Pro" version at a price so low—$19.95—that hardly anyone who needs this kind of product can afford not to buy it. Fookes has no shipping costs; all his software is downloadable online. He outsources credit card processing and site hosting so he can concentrate on his software. This is a "dream" Internet business in almost every way.

Of course, to start a business just like this one you had better be an excellent programmer who writes a piece of software that is one of the best—if not the best—of its kind. Or you had better have a similarly excellent product or service of some sort, and sell it as cleanly as Fookes sells *NoteTab*.

Online Community: Slashdot

The idea of allowing Web users to post directly on your site, with other users then adding comments to the original posts, seems like a "no brainer" money machine on the surface. Instead of paying high salaries to writers and editors, you get a site filled with interesting material for free. Newspaper "letters to the editor" pages are always one of a paper's most-read features, so it seems obvious that the *vox populi's* popularity would transfer both easily and profitably to the Internet.

Merchants—at least merchants who haven't tried to run one—often seem to view company-sponsored online communities as places where happy customers can post glowing product reviews. Computer hardware and software vendors dream of using online communities as a way to cut customer support costs, envisioning experienced users happily helping new users learn how to use the latest piece of hardware or figure out how to get the most from their newest software release.

Managing a large-scale, wide-open community discussion site is a long-hours, high-sweat job. Slashdot (*www.Slashdot.org*), one of the world's largest and best-known discussion sites (see Figure 1–3), has a total of 12 people working on it full-time. Half of them are programmers and sysadmins who spend most of their time trying to protect Slashdot's comment system from incursions by spammers, copyright violators, and others whose hobby is posting off-topic, obscene, or potentially actionable material. There is no shortage of these life forms on the Internet, and if you host a popular discussion forum, they will find you and bother you sooner or

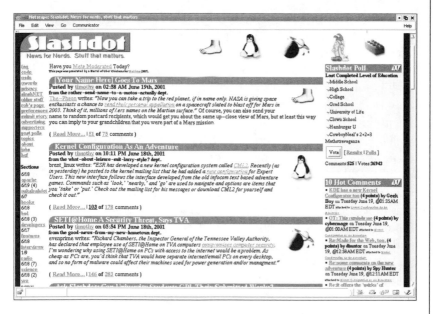

■ **Figure 1–3   Slashdot receives about two
million pageviews on the average weekday.**

later. Count on it. Not only do these posts annoy legitimate readers, but some can lead to legal action. Slashdot routinely receives
requests to have material removed, and has been forced to remove
several readers' posts because of copyright infringement, and to
respond to other allegations through its parent company's lawyer.
So if you plan to operate an "open" online discussion board, in
addition to the cost of editors, moderators, and sysadmins, you had
better put aside a substantial budget reserve for legal defense.

An early, essay-oriented Web site that tried to foster open online
discussion, David Hudson's ReWired (*www.rewired.com*), closed
its discussion area after it got taken over by "script kiddie" hackers
who used ReWired's message boards as a place to exchange information about illegally breaking into computer networks.

Even worse, perhaps, than a discussion board that gets taken
over by undesirables, is one that stays empty week after week.
There are thousands of these out there, attached to all kinds of
Web sites, standing in mute testimony to their owners' failure to
attract the eager hordes of intelligent commentators they obviously expected when they first put up their sites. It's fairly easy to set
up an online discussion board; there are plenty of free or low-cost
software packages around you can use to do it. But then comes the

hard work of nurturing discussions, which is a continuing, labor-intensive task. Sure, Slashdot gets thousands of reader posts daily now, but when it first started it only got a few. Like many "overnight" Web phenomena, it was around and slowly building long before it got any mass media attention, known and inhabited only by a small group of fans who helped define its tone. At the beginning, Slashdot was a hobby site, not a commercial venture, which also helped. Posters didn't feel they were giving away free content to a profit-making corporation, just speaking their minds to others like themselves. A strict focus on leading-edge science and technology and their effects on our culture also helped build Slashdot's popularity; this topic-specific world view gave the site a defined rallying point around which all discussions could revolve, and it was one that was especially well-suited for the technologists and computer science students who made up a majority of Slashdot's early users.

Slashdot, and online discussions in general, deserve a section of their own—and you will find one later in this book. But you'll want to think long and hard before you try to build an online discussion area of any kind yourself, especially if you want it to be part of a site whose main purpose is to sell goods or services. _Amazon.com_ can handle uncomplimentary book reviews because Amazon's income isn't tied to the sale of any one book. A vendor that sells many different makes and models of digital cameras may be willing to post unfavorable reviews of a few of the items it carries, but sooner or later a user is going to ask, "If that particular product is so lousy, why do you carry it?"

This is when, suddenly, the reality of running an open discussion forum attached to an ecommerce site sinks in. Should the vendor remove that dubious post and risk being called a censor who allows only sweetness and light? Should a vendor site's discussion area display only posts that are approved by an employee before they are made visible to the public? That is, should vendors have only "moderated" discussions? Many news sites check submissions and post only those they feel are appropriate in an attempt to enforce some minimal level of propriety, just like a newspaper's "letters" page. Even Slashdot, which allows almost anyone to post almost anything, and doesn't prescreen posts at all, has a moderation system that makes some reader comments easier to see than others.

Think long and hard about the ramifications and pitfalls of running an online community before you try to start one of your own, either as a standalone venture or as part of a news, ecommerce, or

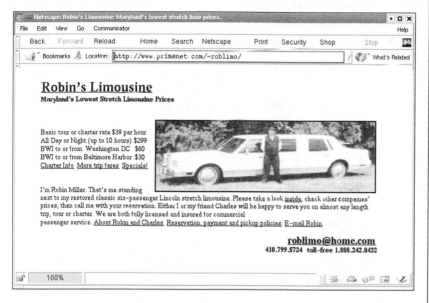

■ **Figure 1–4   The original "million dollar" Robin's Limousine Web site.**

promotional site. In the end, especially after you've read the rest of this book, you may decide you are better off avoiding this particular Web sub-genre altogether.

Brochureware: Robin's Limousine

Figure 1–4 illustrates my own, original "Robin's Limousine" Web site (see Figure 1–4). Don't try the email address or phone number on it. They are obsolete. The site itself has now been replaced by a slightly more sophisticated one, and my old friend and partner, Charles McCoy, now runs the business while I write full-time. I'm using this old snapshot as an example of a site that had no interactive features whatsoever, but was such a successful advertisement that a year after we put it up, Charles and I stopped doing any other paid advertising. We even pulled out of the Yellow Pages.

Web designers and consultants often sneer at simple sites like this as "brochureware." They say this kind of site does nothing that couldn't be done just as well on paper. They're right. But often the objective of a small or local business's Web site is exactly the same as that of a printed brochure: to get the potential customer to pick up the phone and call. The Internet, in this case, is being used as nothing but a means of delivering a brochure to someone who might not otherwise find out about the business. The actual sale takes place over the phone or in person, depending on the kind of business. My little limo Web site, which cost literally nothing to make (aside from a few hours of my time) and was hosted by my ISP as part of an "unlimited Internet access" package that cost $16.95, total, per month when I first signed up for it, has generated at least $1 million in business since it first went up in 1994. This is an amazing return on investment, but one that other small business owners can easily duplicate.

One of the two big reasons my limo site was so successful was its simplicity. While my competitors were adding glitzy features to their sites that either made them take forever to download through dialup modems or made them unviewable through many Web browsers, mine was easily viewed with any kind of computer or browser through any connection. The other reason the site succeeded so well was careful placement in search engines and (free) limo industry and local online business directory listings. Any business, of any size, should try to make its Web site as easy to view— and as easy to find—as possible. I am continually shocked when I see major company Web sites that work correctly on only one or two types of computer operating systems or Web-browsing software, and are not listed appropriately in search engines and directories. You would think they'd know better. But apparently they don't. Oh, well.

A Web Site Is Not a Business

The one thing which all the examples I have just shown have in common is that the Web sites themselves are not trying to be businesses, but are used as ways to *facilitate* business. Wired News and Slashdot, for example, sell advertising; on the surface they look as if they exist to provide news and information to their readers, but the main *business* of these sites is selling ads. That's where their money comes from. Many online publishers that started in the mid- or late 1990s didn't seem to realize what business they were in, and built staffs larger than any amount of ad revenue they could possibly generate would ever support. Most members of this crowd have either gone broke, gotten acquired, or are limping along and hoping for miracles that probably aren't going to happen.

On the ecommerce front, *MexGrocer.com*'s owners know full well they are in the business of selling non-perishable food, not in the Web site business. Ignacio Hernandez, who runs it, sold wholesale Mexican food products "the old fashioned way" for over 30 years before there was an Internet. His son, *MexGrocer.com* Vice President Ignacio Hernandez, Jr., worked for an online grocery company in Switzerland before coming home to work in the family business. *MexGrocer.com* was started with no outside venture capital. No immediate investment in warehouses or delivery infrastructure was required because the Hernandez family had already been in the grocery distribution business for three generations in Mexico and the United States.

For the Hernadez family, a Web site serves two simple purposes: It is a low-cost way to reach customers that might otherwise not buy from them, and it makes ordering more convenient—and lowers order processing costs—for existing wholesale customers. These are entirely reasonable expectations. The Hernandezes may not get rich overnight from an IPO, but *MexGrocer.com* is being built on a permanent foundation that gives it a fair chance of earning a steady profit, not only for its current operators but for future Hernandez generations.

Contrast this with *Pets.com*, a company that was founded as a pure ecommerce venture in 1998, raised $82.5 million in a public offering in February, 2000, and closed its virtual doors in November, 2000. *Pets.com* had a much slicker Web site than *MexGrocer.com* and probably spent more on advertising in its short life than the Hernandez family has spent in any whole decade. But *Pets.com* had no retail, warehouse, delivery, or manufacturing capability to build on when it started. In essence, *Pets.com* was nothing but a Web site. The *Pets.com* URL now directs users to *PETsMART.com*, the online affiliate of "brick-and-mortar" chain pet supplies retailer PETsMART, which has been around and growing steadily since 1987.

When I first started advertising my limo service online in 1994, I already had established contacts among local hotel concierges, wedding planners, and others who could and did help me find customers. I owned an old (but impeccably maintained) six-passenger Lincoln stretch limousine, and had the insurance and licenses I needed to operate as a commercial transporter in Maryland. Between 1993 and 1996, at least 1000 entrepreneurs tried to start online limo booking or marketing systems of one sort or another, either local, national, or international. They all wanted to charge limo operators either monthly fees or commissions in return for getting bookings for them. One of the old jokes in the limousine industry is that it would be a perfect business if you could just eliminate its three main headaches: vehicles, drivers, and customers. That's essentially what all the online limo booking entrepreneurs tried to do, but almost all of them are gone now. New ones keep springing up and disappearing, too. The only limo Web sites that seem to stick around, and the only ones that seem to make any money, are those run by limo operators who actually own (and carefully maintain) limousines, deal directly with customers, and have real, live drivers working for them.

The Difference between an Online Business and an Online Hobby

Whether you are an individual entrepreneur or work for a multi-national corporation, building a Web site with no concrete goal in mind is a hobby that probably won't generate any profit. Yes, some sites that are now popular, and some that are profitable, began as hobbies, but most Internet businesses that were founded during the Age of Internet Euphoria (roughly 1994–2000) with high hopes and shaky business plans (or no business plans at all) are now either dead or on their way out. A very few, including eBay, Yahoo!, and Slashdot, that started out as part-time labors of love, are still alive and doing fine, but for every one of these there are thousands that never made a dime.

There is nothing wrong with creating a hobby or vanity Web site that isn't expected to make money. If that's what you want, go ahead and make it, but do it with your eyes open. Putting up a Web site and getting a lot of people to look at it is fun, but without a way to turn all those pageviews into more cash than it costs to run the site, you'll end up in the same pickle Disney got into with its first online operation. Remember their highly-touted _Go.com_ that debuted in 1998? Millions of people used _Go.com_ as it grew from a simple and highly-regarded search engine into a general-purpose Web portal that tried to compete with Yahoo!, Excite, and all the rest of those beasts even though _Go.com_ had neither a clearly defined focus nor, apparently, any sensible plan to make money.

Early in 2001, the Disney Internet Group ceased operating as a separate business unit, laid off 400 employees, and forced its parent, The Walt Disney Company, to take a total write-off estimated at over $800 million. Talk about an expensive hobby!

Can you (or your company) afford to do as Disney did, even on a smaller scale? I didn't think so.

But that's enough generalities. Let's move on to the specifics of building a focused, user-friendly, *profitable* Web site.

Building a Web Site that Works

A frightfully large percentage of commercial Web sites are poorly designed, implemented, and maintained. In 1993 or 1994, when we were all just learning how to make a site, and Web browsers were so primitive that they could hardly do more than display a single column of text and a picture or two, poor site design was understandable. Today there is no excuse for it. There is a huge body of literature available on the subject. Those serious about making money on the Internet, on any level, should spend some time familiarizing themselves with usability issues and what they can and cannot do with HTML, XML, Javascript, and other basic Web design technologies.

Avoiding the Worst Mistakes

The list of common Web site errors is so long that it's hard to know where to start, so let's begin with a few of the most egregious ones in no particular order:

Broken links. When readers or customers see broken links on your site, you look like you don't care about your business. It's the same as telling you to turn to page 620 in this book when there is no page 620. Instant credibility meltdown! There are many simple ways to redirect outdated links either to your front page or, perhaps better, to a specific page that tells readers why a particular page is no longer there, with instructions on how to find similar material elsewhere on your site. Of course, this should be necessary only for readers coming to your site through links from search engines or other referring sites. You should never have any bad links of your own—that is, links on your site leading to dead pages.

Making readers jump through hoops to get to the "meat" of your site's message. If you are running a news site, the first thing a reader should see, front and center, is news. If you are selling goods or services, your offerings should be top dead center. The worst thing you can give a new reader is a message that says, "You need the latest version of AudioIntruder installed to take full advantage of this site's features. Download it <u>here.</u>" Huh? We just want to read an article or price some merchandise, not download software. So we readers click away when we see that message. There are plenty of other Web sites that work fine with software we already have. We also don't need to see mission statements, cute animated introductions, or any other time-wasters before you give us the information we want. (You can use all the animation and other cute tricks you want somewhere or other on your site, as long as you don't force them down our throats on your first page, okay?)

Bad navigation schemes. Your site can be full of wonderful copy and great art, but if site visitors can't find all this goodness, every bit of effort and money you put into your creation is wasted. Sure, you can find your way around your Web site. But what about the rest of us, the people who have never seen your site before or come to it only when we're in the market for your products or looking for specific information? Wouldn't you rather have us concentrating on what you have to offer than groping around trying to find it? We are not going to put a lot of effort into rooting around on your site, looking for half-hidden information, before we go back to a search engine and try to find something similar elsewhere.

Crashing readers' browsers. This is the worst Web site sin you can commit. Browser crashes are usually caused by bad

Javascript or poor code generated by Microsoft Front Page or other "easy" Web site creation software. Writing HTML, Java, and Javascript takes skill, and the more complicated a site's HTML, Java, and Javascript get, the more skill it takes to make everything work right. (If you or your hired Web designer don't know how to make a complex site that will work with almost any Web browser, get a new Web designer—or make a simpler site.)

Take Pity on Phone Modem Users. You may have a broadband Net connection at your office, but over 80% of U.S. Internet users and up to 95% of all Internet users worldwide use telephone modems that can take minutes, not seconds, to download a Web page full of large graphics and complicated HTML formatting. A page that takes much more than 10 seconds to load will drive most users away — and you can't think that because a phone modem is "supposed" to work at 56K and handle 56KB per second that a page with a total of 560KB worth of information will load in 10 seconds. Depending on the page's file structure, and the actual, real life speed of your potential customer's connection, which may be closer to 21K than 56K for all you know, you may be forcing that customer to wait as long as two minutes to view that page. Of course, after 10 or 20 seconds, she's probably going to click away from your site, never to return.

There are many other evils inflicted on the Web-using public by clueless designers and site owners, but the ones listed above are the worst of the worst. Now that we've got them spotted, we'll look at ways to make a good site, starting with its basic architecture and moving into just enough technical detail to show why some sites work well (and are popular) and others don't work well (and are either unpopular or not as popular as they could be with a little reworking).

Information Layering

This phrase may be new to you, but information layering is used in one way or another by almost every successful Web site. It's a technique you can use easily on the Web, only with great difficulty in

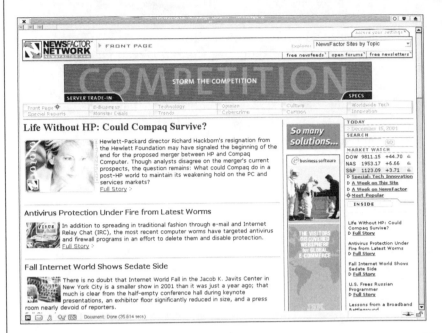

Figure 2–1   NewsFactor Network home page.

print, and not at all in broadcast media. Describing the concept in theory would take thousands of words, but a few pictures will make it clear in seconds, so that's what we'll use.

NewFactor Network (see Figure 2–1) makes excellent use of information layering. Here's the front page (Figure 2–1), with the first paragraph of each current general interest story on the site showing, along with an attractive (but small) graphic related to each story. Beyond the general interest reporting, a click on one of the links below the top of this page will take you to one of the site's many special interest sections. *Cybercrime* is a page that may not appeal to everyone, but it contains vital information for security-conscious NewsFactor readers.

This page (see Figure 2–2) goes much deeper into Internet and security matters than the main NewsFactor page; some stories from it may appear on the main page, but many security and cyber-crime-related stories appear only in this section. This use of infor-mation layering means NewsFactor main page readers, who may want to scan only a few headlines that relate to Internet business in general, don't have a lot of specialized crime-related stories inflicted on them, but still catch the highlights of the *CyberCrime* section, and those who are interested specifically in security and

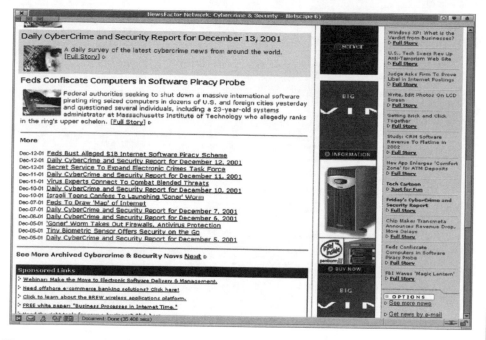

■ **Figure 2–2   Part of NewsFactor Network's**
CyberCrime section page.

crime still have a wealth of information available to them from
NewsFactor Network.

Here's a portion of NewsFactor Network's *Industry Trends* page
(see Figure 2–3). There isn't a word about security matters in sight.
The articles here are aimed at an audience primarily interested in
marketing and business strategy.

Note that all of these pages, like the main and section head
pages on almost all successful news Web sites, show only story
headlines and a short summary of each story's content. Once again,
this is information layering. Headline-scanning readers have the
option of reading only those stories that interest them and ignor-
ing the rest.

Here's yet another information layer, one that is at the bottom
of every NewsFactor story: a set of hyperlinks (see Figure 2–4).
One link is to a talkback section where readers can discuss the
story. Below that, there's a group of links to *Related Stories* for
readers who want more information about the main story's topic
than it contained directly. And the third group of links is to advertising pages that may be of specific interest to people who chose to
read an article about (in this case) the possibility of new programs

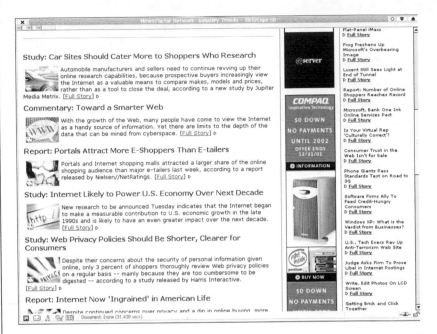

Figure 2–3   NewsFactor Network's *Industry Trends* page.

under development that may someday browse the Internet and trade data without any direct human intervention.

Each NewsFactor reader gets just as much or as little information as he or she wants, and each new layer of information is easy to reach from the one that is above it.

Information layering may be a new phrase, but the idea behind it has been used by librarians as long as there have been libraries with books (or before that, scrolls or stone tablets) filed in categories and sub-categories. One of the Web's great strengths is the ease with which pieces of information can be linked to each other, either from one site to another or within a single site. In effect, hyperlinks can act as footnotes (and footnotes to footnotes) without the layout problems that footnotes create in printed books.

The closest a newspaper could come to information layering would be to have a front page with nothing but headlines, brief story summaries, and cumbersome "turn to page XX for more" notes all over it. Television and radio, because of their necessarily linear information delivery system, cannot use information layering at all; the only way a broadcaster can use information layering is to put up a Web site and refer viewers or listeners to it.

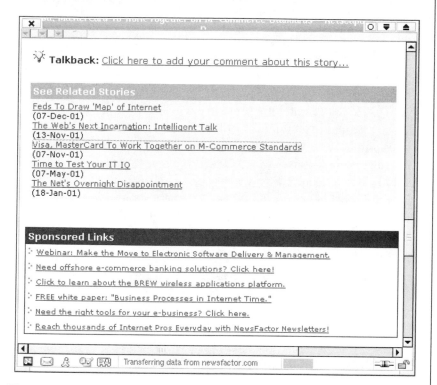

Figure 2–4 Links at the bottom of each NewsFactor story lead to yet more information layers.

A Web site that is not built from the start to use information layering is not taking full advantage of the Internet. It is tempting, especially for people who have cut their media or marketing teeth offline, to deliver Web content the same way it is delivered in print or via broadcast media, but on a fiercely competitive Internet, those who try to do this are doomed to lose out to people who make full use of the Internet's capabilities instead of trying to pretend it is something it is not.

Although NewsFactor Network was built by people with prior offline journalism and marketing experience, it was designed from the start as an Internet-based content and advertising delivery system, easy for readers to use, and easy (hence inexpensive) for editors and reporters to manage from the "back end" of the site. It was not an accidental phenomenon started by a pair of college students in their dorm room, but a conscious effort by professionals to build a site that would attract not just one targeted audience, but a whole series of differentiated audience groups which a wide range of tech-oriented advertisers would pay premium rates to reach. Expenses have been held down brutally so that even during advertising downturns the site maintains a positive cash flow.

This success is repeatable. Not by copying NewsFactor Network, but by using the same level of ingenuity, planning, and hard work that went into it—and by using information layering cleverly from the moment you start thinking about making (or redesigning) your site, not only as a way to make your site attractive to readers but as a way to hold down content and bandwidth costs by giving each individual reader only the information he or she wants instead of acting like a newspaper and delivering every bit of information you publish to every single reader.

Basic Web Design Usability Rules

This Web stuff is not brand-new anymore. We have enough experience with it that we can come up with rules that make a site easy for readers to use and understand. Here are some of the most basic ones:

- All underlined words are links, and all text links consist of underlined words.

- Your site's logo or title (or company name or company logo) should appear on every page, and clicking on that logo or title must take a user back to your home page.

- All small pictures (thumbnails) that refer to stories or catalog items on your site should be links to the stories or items pictured unless they are part of the story or catalog page itself, in which case they should link to larger, clearer versions of the thumbnails.

- Every picture on your site should directly relate to its content. If you are selling computers, show pictures of the computers you are selling, not generic cartoon computers or stock photos of business-attired people shaking hands.

- Each individual Web page must have its own URL (i.e., *www.buildprofitsonline.com/rules*) so that readers can bookmark *that particular page* for future reference.

- Don't use frames. Search engines can't read through them, and without a lot of fancy dancing in the code behind them, frames make it almost impossible for readers to bookmark a single page within your site.

- Avoid "splash" pages that say nothing but "Welcome to our Web site" or something similar. The first page a new site visitor sees should have information, not platitudes, on it.

- Do not force readers to use Flash, RealPlayer, or other browser plugin software to view your site's main page or any of its essential contents. Ever. If you do this, you instantly lose every reader who does not have the right plugin (and the right version of that plugin) installed.

- Remember that there are many browsers and operating systems out there. Just because you use Linux and the latest Mozilla browser doesn't mean that all your potential readers do. Some may use Microsoft Internet Explorer on a Mac, others may use Opera or Netscape on a computer running Windows. View your site design through as many different browsers, on as many different operating systems, as you possibly can. At the very least, make sure your site displays correctly in the three or four most popular browsers, on computers running Linux, Mac, and Windows.

When In Doubt, Steal

Hopefully, if you're planning to make or remake a Web site, you're spending a fair amount of time looking at other sites, deciding what works and what doesn't. Take notes while you do this research; make detailed notes about site features that work for you and about features that give you heartburn.

Perhaps you like the "liquid layout" of _ThinkGeek.com_ that allows it to look good in a browser window over 1000 pixels wide (see Figure 2–5) and equally fine in a window only 650 pixels wide (see Figure 2–6).

Whenever you notice a useful site feature that you like, make a note. And note that "liquid layout" that automatically adjusts a Web site's layout to match different browser window sizes is a good thing in general; browser windows can vary, depending on monitor size and individual preference, from as small as 500 pixels wide to over 1000, although the most common minimum width for a displayed Web page is now generally considered to be 750 pixels; if

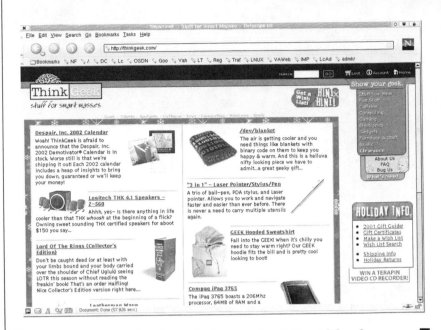

Figure 2–5   ThinkGeek shown the full width of a typical 15-inch monitor screen: 1024 pixels wide.

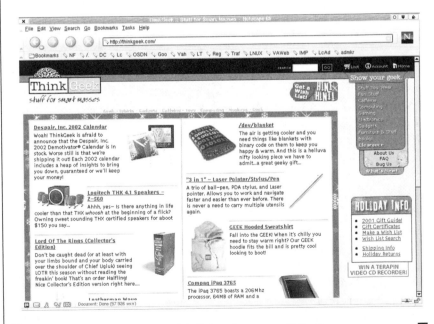

Figure 2–6   Same ThinkGeek page, this time in a browser window only 650 pixels wide.

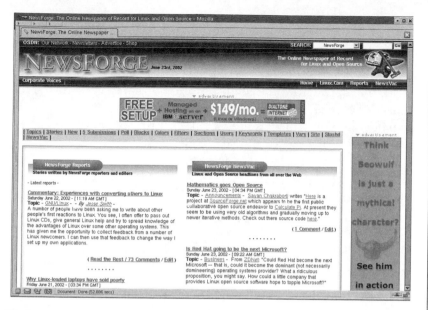

Figure 2–7   Top of the _NewsForge.com_ front page.

your site requires a minimum browser window wider than that, it is going to be hard to read for people who have standard 14-inch or 15-inch monitors running at their default resolutions.

Now go look at another site. If you're making an advertiser-supported news site, perhaps you like the way NewsForge (see Figure 2–7) carries its most prominent banner ad under the masthead instead of in the more typical top-of-the-page position. Write that idea down too.

Wander around the Web, jotting down not only site features you like but also ones you don't like. Then show your list to co-workers and friends. Maybe they have other little tricks and features they've spotted that you'll want to add to your list. Maybe some of the features you like turn others off for one reason or another, and you'll want to remove them from your list. Between you and your advisors, you are also likely to come up with a substantial list of both "good" and "bad" site features.

Obviously, when you make your site, you are going to want to use as many of the features on the "good" list as you can, and you are going to want to avoid everything you have on your "don't do this" list, but what's a little less obvious is that you can happily "steal" most of the design and navigation features you and your associates liked—and incorporate them into your site design.

The trick to online feature-stealing is to *not* do what TV programming executives do when they directly copy last year's hit shows; instead of taking one site's entire concept and design and trying to duplicate it, try to find a few bits here and a piece or two there that appeal to you, then use those bits and pieces as inspirations. If you make a site that looks just like Yahoo!, and does pretty much the same thing as the original, why would anyone want to use your site instead of the real thing? There are plenty of bar bands that can play every Rolling Stones song note for note—but will never be as popular as Mick Jagger and crew. Bands that get beyond the local scene almost always do it with their own original music, staging, and performance style.

It is possible to steal plenty, and still turn out an original work. William Shakespeare stole most of his plots, and at last look some of his plays were still reasonably popular hundreds of years after they were written.

Selecting Web Designers

One advantage of making a "features I would like to steal" list is that it makes dealing with a hired Web designer much easier. Saying, "I want to have folders along the left side just like the ones on DaveCentral," and showing them *DaveCentral.com* to see what you mean, is less confusing to your designer than trying to describe the functions of those folders verbally or by email.

But before you get to that point with a Web designer, you need to select one. In-house? An outside contractor? Your nephew who is good with computers? Do it by yourself, on your own, because you know how to write a little HTML—or because you're willing to learn how to write HTML and how to deal with Cascading Style Sheets and all that? It's a hard choice, and it depends on the size of your company, your budget, and the amount of time you have available.

In most corporate situations, you are likely to have either an in-house Web designer or some sort of relationship with an outside ad agency or Web design firm already, and if you suddenly bring in a consultant or other outsider, egos will be bent. You may even find that the marketing executives or other individuals who were in charge of your company's Web site development before you took over, and not the designers themselves, are to blame for your

Hiring Programmers for Your Web Site

Hire full-time programmers to work on your Web site only if it is part of an integrated software package that is running your entire business or if your site is so large and changes so often that it needs constant backend work. Even in these situations, you probably don't need a full-time programmer dedicated to nothing but your Web site, but will be better off having several members of your in-house programming team work on it so that you won't be left high and dry in case one quits.

You should not pay to have custom software written; there are plenty of Open Source content management, ecommerce, and database packages already out there that can easily be modified to fit your specific requirements. (Turn to Chapter 8 for reasons why you should stick to Open Source software instead of buying proprietary programs.)

You should also beware of letting programmers "drive" your project. Your Web site is supposed to be a resource for your readers or customers, not a guaranteed employment program for software developers. You hire programmers, like Web designers, to do what *you* need done, not to do what *they* want to do. The high demand for Web-hip programmers in 1997–2000 led many of them into the trap of believing they could do anything they wanted, and if they ran into a boss who didn't cave in to their every demand, they could go around the corner and get a better job or consulting gig in a few minutes. Now we are starting to see a more rational marketplace, especially for programmers who specialize in Java, CGI, Perl, PHP, and other languages useful for making Web sites.

If you are not a current or former programmer yourself, or do not have extensive experience hiring and managing programmers, you may be better off hiring an outside development firm to make your Web site. It doesn't need to be a big or famous company. Indeed, you are more likely to get good service at a fair price from a smaller firm. When you come right down to it, what you are hiring when you contract out your work is a programmer or two and a designer or two, not the support staff, slick brochures, account executives, and fancy offices with elegant conference rooms that big Web design firms use to impress you. The only real factors you should consider when hiring either individual programmers and designers or a firm selling Web design and programming services are portfolio quality, willingness to work closely with you, and price. If you get the best combination of these three factors from three talented people jammed into a basement home office, go with them, smile at the money you're saving, and don't worry about their lack of slick digs. Nobody looking at your Web site will know or care about anything besides how it looks and works.

One major request you must make of anyone who works on your site, whether they are in-house employees, individual free-lancers, or an outside design firm, is adequate documentation, up to and including (at least for sites with more than a dozen pages) flow charts and other illustrations that describe the site's navigation scheme and interactions between the various bits of code that make your site work. Without clear documentation it can be almost impossible to fire the original person or company and bring in someone new to take over your site's maintenance; in other words, without a "manual" for your site, you will have locked yourself into total dependence on a single supplier, and this is as unhealthy in Web design and programming as it is in any other phase of your business.

Small entrepreneurs building Web sites must be especially careful about getting locked into sole-supplier relationships with Web service providers. Those deals where "We do all the design, hosting, and promotion so you don't have to worry about it" may seem attractive when you see the pitch online (or even in a TV infomercial), but what if that provider goes out of business? Your Web site will disappear and you will be screwed. The only sure way to keep from having this happen— and it's not a remote possibility; applications service providers and Web service companies go out of business, merge or get acquired quite frequently—is to maintain total control over your site, from domain name on.

company's underperforming Web site. If this is the case—as it so often is—you need to repair the existing relationship, not look for a new one.

Dealing with Web designers when you are not one yourself is like traveling in a foreign country; even if you speak only a little bit of the local language and have a rotten accent, the fact that you are trying to speak and understand the native tongue at all will get you better service and make you more friends than if you arrogantly expect every person you meet to speak English, German, or whatever other language you speak at home. A few hours spent looking through some of the design-oriented books and Web sites listed in the "Resources" section at the back of this book *before* you choose a Web designer (or create a relationship with one already on your company's payroll) will pay off heavily later in time and money saved—and in higher quality output.

The first thing to do when evaluating Web designers (now that you know a little of their lingo) is to look at their design portfolios. You are not looking for sites that look exactly the way you want yours to look, just evidence of overall competence. You want to check basic mechanics. Do all the links on the sites they show you work? Are their navigation schemes sensible? Do their color choices and fonts look reasonable to you?

Beware of excessive download times and monitor requirements. If you have a high-speed Net connection and a 21-inch monitor at work, and a small laptop and phone modem connection at home, you may want to view prospective designers' work at home before making a final decision. You should certainly view all samples in more than one browser on more than one type of computer, which may take time and trouble but is worth the extra effort every time. Another test is to print out a few pages. Do they look coherent on paper? The value of a print test may not be immediately apparent, but when you look at the way people and companies make buying decisions, you'll realize that many Web users may want to print out a few pages from your site now and then and look at them on paper or pass them around before making a major buying decision, so you want to make this as easy as possible for your prospective customers.

There is also the intangible matter of rapport. An old military truism states, "A merely competent squad machine gunner whom you know and trust is better than one who is a perfect shot, but whom you don't trust." When you hire a Web designer to make a site for you, it is still *your* site. Yes, the designer is a professional (we hope!) who knows more about his or her job than you do, but you know your business and your customers better than anyone else (we hope!) so you must make the final decisions about how your Web site should look and feel. Your Web designer must be able to accept this. Yes, he or she is entitled to your respect, and you should not reject suggestions from your designer out of hand without good reason, but the chain of command must be firmly established from the start.

And then there is the putative "nephew who knows the Internet" to whom so many small entrepreneurs turn for Web site design help. There is nothing wrong with having a friend, co-worker or family member who is not a professional Web designer make a site for you, as long as it is a simple site consisting of fewer than 10 or 12 pages. A big site, especially one for an ecommerce venture that is essentially an online catalog with hundreds or thousands of items listed, is as much of a database structuring job as it is a design job per se, so your friend or relative had better be familiar with database structures before you turn him or her loose on your Web site. But then, if you are doing a site of any scale, you ought to be able to budget enough money to hire a competent and experienced designer. If you can't afford a professional designer, you may want to scale back your plans, at least at the beginning. That said, there is nothing inherently wrong with having a friend or relative design a simple site for you, but do not expect too much from someone without experience, or you are sure to be disappointed.

One last word on hiring a Web designer: You will not get competent work from someone who uses Microsoft FrontPage or one of the other site design programs that supposedly turn out "instant" Web pages. These programs are like instant coffee; they are simply not as good as the real thing. Make sure that any designer you hire thoroughly understands HTML, XML, or any other code your site requires, and isn't faking it.

Dealing with Hired Web Designers

A truism in the computer industry goes, "Just because a programmer *can* do something doesn't mean he *should* do it." The same applies to Web site design.

There are, for example, many ways to make text on your site blink, fade, rotate, or otherwise move around. It is easy to make images jump from one side of a reader's screen to the other. It can be tempting to add sound files to a site so that every time a reader clicks on your main page, he or she gets not only words and pictures, but background music, too. Every one of these devices will irritate more readers than they will attract.

The purpose of a commercial Web site is to convey information, either in the form of news that will attract many readers so that you can sell enough advertising or subscriptions to make a profit, or information about products and services you are selling yourself. Either way, you want no gizmos or gimmicks on your site that will detract from its main message.

Music? Very nice idea, but don't force it down people's throats. Many of us use our computers as CD or MP3 players while we check Web sites, so we aren't going to hear it anyway. Other users may be in office settings where music without warning may be considered rude by co-workers. So if you or your Web designer want to provide music, do it with a "background music" icon which users can click if they want to listen, and ignore if they don't.

Flash animation? Web designers often fall in love with Flash because it gives them a chance to show off groovy graphics and movements and sound without using as much bandwidth as other methods of sending video and audio over the Internet. The only problem is that Flash will detract from your message more often than not. Sure, you can include little bits of Flash here and there to spice things up, or perhaps a Flash product demonstration or two, but don't overdo it. If your designer is a Flash hotshot, he or she can put up his or her own site that displays nothing but Flash artwork, much the same way a graphics artist who lays out newspaper ads for car dealers by day may do wild abstract paintings at night.

Blinking, fading, and rotating text were fun when they were brand-new—in 1994. Now they are nothing but cheap tricks. An artfully selected headline font will deliver your message better.

As a general rule, the more experienced a Web designer you hire, the fewer gimmicks he or she will try to stick on your site. This is yet another reason you (hopefully) hired a Web designer with provable skills and a strong portfolio.

Web designers need to be treated with respect, and you need to gain theirs as well if you want to get good work out of them on time and under budget. You get their respect by telling them, clearly, exactly what you do and don't want on your site, and why. You gain more respect by soliciting their input on how you can best accomplish your goals than by micromanaging them, and you can take that respect to an even higher level by asking these skilled professionals if they have ideas that might be better than yours that will save money or make things better and easier for your users.

All this discussion needs to take place before anyone actually starts working on your site beyond the rough sketch level. The single most expensive thing you can do while building (or rebuilding) a Web site is make major changes to a project half-way or two-thirds of the way through.

You must decide, before you get going, exactly what your site will and won't contain, how it is going to look, and how users are going to navigate it. And once those decisions are made, you must stick to them even if you—or your designer or your programmer or someone else—have a whole bunch of brilliant new ideas after work on your site has started.

You may want to read the preceding sentence several times. More Web projects have probably been ruined, both in the budget sense and esthetically, by in-process changes than by any other single factor, and management mind-changing is one of the greatest problems cited by Web designers and programmers when dealing with non-technical bosses.

Web designers are, by definition, task-oriented people. They want to know exactly what they are supposed to do, then go do it without a lot of fumbling around. Many people who go into this field do not have good social skills, so they may not be able to express their displeasure with management failures as easily as people in more outgoing professions, but this doesn't mean the displeasure isn't there—and that it won't show up in the form of work that isn't as good as it could or should be. It is up to you, as the person with overall responsibility for the site, to provide firm direction from the very start and to maintain a straight course as the project develops, no matter how many interesting detours or new routes present themselves along the way.

Maintaining Site Focus

If you have a news site, deliver news. If you have an ecommerce site, do nothing but sell. If your site is supposed to promote a business, promote like mad on every page, with every word and picture on the entire site.

During the latter part of the Net's initial boom-spasm, an awful lot of people running ecommerce and promotional sites decided they needed news of some sort on their sites in order to increase traffic. Some of them paid professional journalists thousands of dollars to write daily, weekly, or monthly columns. These sponsored news pages were great for the writers and editors who got

As part of the research for this book, I turned to users of Jeffrey Zeldman's *A List Apart* Web site (*www.alistapart.com*) for advice. This is one of the most-respected online gathering spots for, as the site's tagline says, "people who make Web sites."

I asked *A List Apart* members to share their pet client peeves with me. Boy, did I get an earful!

Selected quotes follow:

"Nothing worse than launching a site and then having to go back and revise it umpteen zillion times (especially when graphics are involved)."

"Word to the wise: beware the client who says 'that price is too much,' then refuses to say what *isn't* too much."

"Do not expect that we will work for free. We do not update your site for you for free. We do not make extra banners for you for free. We are not your technical support. We do not know why your computer crashed. (Or if we do, it's not our job to tell you.)"

"Shop around and be up-front about it. It takes time in the beginning, but it will pay off in the long run. Follow the business rule of thumb of getting three quotes. We do it for our other business decisions, but somehow forget when it comes to the Web."

"*Check references.* Get a good vibe from current and past clients. You wouldn't hire an employee without checking references, so do the same with your developer."

"I find that a lot of clients want dynamic sites that are fresh. However, they haven't considered who will manage and create content. This task will be part of someone's job description, will take some time, and the content manager will need to be supported. We can build some great things, but we can't write your manager's daily message for you. I have seen many a great application gather dust because it is no one's responsibility to maintain it."

"The common denominator in any design discipline is communication. Rubbish in, rubbish out."

"Don't make me build you a high-bandwidth Flash intro for a site whose audience is mostly modem users."

"...if these 'net business owners want everything for free or a professional, customized, e-commerce Web site done for less than $500, please tell them to quit their business and go work for someone else who runs a real business. A $200 Web site is *not* going to be successful."

"I wish clients would concentrate on the question, 'What do I really have to offer?' instead of worrying about the way that stuff will be presented best."

"I don't care if the project is your baby, if the CEO is the only one who can approve the deliverables, she should be present at a planning meeting. I know she's busy. So am I. I'll work around her schedule the best I possibly can, but trying to develop a site with no input from the person I'm ultimately going to have to please is like driving a car with a blindfold on. Coming back to me after the final deliverables have been presented for acceptance and saying 'Well, the strategy has changed' or 'The CEO wants these changes' doesn't cut it. I don't get to tell my landlord that I'm not paying rent this month because the CEO didn't approve it, you don't get a free redesign because you didn't get the CEO's approval before giving me the go-ahead to proceed."

I got over 100 responses on *A List Apart* from professional Web developers who want to do great work but feel their clients hold them back. A recurring complaint not included above because it was expressed in words that would be improper in this book, was about clients who were late with copy or pictures for their sites, but expected developers to meet the timetable on which both parties had originally agreed anyway. Another theme was client changes; just as book printers charge to reset type once clients have approved their copy in final "galley" form, Web developers charge for changes made to finished sites, and get irritated when customers feel they should redo work for free.

Site maintenance was another sore point, with more than a few developers upset that clients who tried to insert new text or modify old text on their sites accidentally messed up the HTML code and ruined carefully-designed layouts. There are, of course, many ways to set up a Web site so that copy expected to change frequently can be entered easily by anyone who knows how to use a text editor and a Web browser, but like everything else about a Web site, a designer will include this feature only if a client requests it in advance because it is cheaper and easier to build a site on plain-Jane HTML than to include back-end forms for future text insertion.

There were also notes about clients who hired a professional designer, then overruled their design decisions for reasons such as "blue is my favorite color, so use a lot of blue." Contracts generated a whole separate discussion thread; it seems many Web designers have been burned by not getting written contracts from clients detailing their exact tasks and payment terms. There was consensus that clients who want to pay "after the site starts to turn a profit" instead of putting up a 30% or 50% deposit in advance, with the balance upon completion, are almost always blowing smoke, and should be avoided.

An awful lot of the speed bumps boiled down to poor communication between Web developers and their clients, with one side of the table as often at fault as the other. This is why I stress the impor- tance of throwing ideas back and forth and getting everything settled before the design work starts, instead of sitting back and saying, "Do whatever you want," then having the whole project redone after the fact—almost certainly at your expense—because it didn't turn out the way you expected.

paid to make them, but probably did nothing to increase anyone's sales. Now that the Net is settling down, this idea is gradually going away. This is bad for writers who have lost a source of easy money, but so it goes. The good ones will find other gigs, and the not-so-good ones will drift into public relations, time-share condominium sales, TV infomercial production, or some other field that gives them money without requiring hard physical labor in return.

Sure, doing away with extraneous writing was usually a budget-cutting move, with renewed site focus merely a side effect. But in this case the side effect is marvelously serendipitous; when you have potential customers on your site, you want them to concentrate on *buying*. You don't want to distract them with news any more than you want to distract them with whirling logos or background music. The original Sears, Roebuck catalog—which begat modern mail order; which begat telephone ordering; which begat ecommerce—had no news in it. Customers ordered from it because it offered plain and easy-to-understand descriptions of the merchandise, along with vivid product illustrations and a simple ordering system. That catalog was a pure selling machine, cover-to-cover.

There are plenty of independent news sources on the Internet, so shoppers are unlikely to turn to a corporate promo or ecommerce site for news. Conversely, news sites that get involved in ecommerce beyond selling t-shirts with their site's name on them or similar impulse-purchase items that are directly related to the site in some way take a chance of tainting the objectivity of their news product or, at the very least, losing the appearance of impartiality in their coverage. And on the Internet, where the news business is probably more competitive than in any other medium, this can be the kiss of death for a news Web site.

During Yahoo!'s period of greatest growth, and for much of the time it was a profitable company, it was primarily a Web directory and search service. Now Yahoo! is trying to do many things at once, and is having trouble making money at most of them. Google (*www.google.com*), a site that is nothing but a search and information-finding service, is not only gaining popularity at a rapid rate, but started showing profits in 2001.

Once again, the "Keep It Simple, Stupid" principle applies: A Web site that does one thing well is more likely to succeed than one that tries to do too much. If you want to run an ecommerce business, promote an unrelated offline business, and deliver online news, that's fine—as long as you do it on three separate sites, with separate domain names, instead of trying to do everything under a single banner.

Profitable
Ecommerce

L et's start by defining ecommerce as "selling goods or services directly over the Internet that are delivered individually to each customer." This definition is important, because there are many businesses that cannot benefit directly from ecommerce and would do better using the Internet as a purely promotional medium and making their actual sales offline, either by phone or in person.

Used cars are an example of products that should not be sold (or bought) online. New, factory-built cars of a given make, model, and color may be essentially identical to one another, but each used car is an individual item, with its potential value determined almost as much by the way it was treated by previous owners as by the characteristics it had when it left the factory. A person who buys a used car without looking it over carefully, driving it, checking under it for fluid leaks, and perhaps having it inspected by a third-party mechanic, is a fool. A car dealer may put up a Web site that shows its used car inventory, but that site should be considered a promotional tool designed to bring prospective customers to the dealer's place of business, not a sales vehicle in and of itself. That dealer needs a *promotional* Web site, not an *ecommerce* site.

This distinction is important enough to give each site its own chapter to avoid confusion.

Now that we've decided what we're talking about here, let's start by saying: "A Web site is a Web site, and all the usability rules we've talked about apply to ecommerce sites as much as they apply to any other kind."

Sell without Shame

One of the worst mental barriers online merchants need to overcome is a belief, possibly subconscious, that it is somehow uncool to make strong, direct sales pitches on the World Wide Web. This probably dates back to 1994, when the Internet first allowed commercial activity and most people online had some sort of academic or government affiliation, and hardly anyone expected to make money from running a Web site. Many of the first unabashedly commercial sites drew open hostility from the "original" Internet denizens, while commercial sites that offered (or at least purportedly offered) some sort of educational or entertainment value in addition to pitching products or services got fewer negative emails than ones that obviously existed only to make money. Times have changed. The vast majority of Web users today came online after 1995 and are accustomed to seeing Web sites that are metaphorical "storefronts" that have "shopping cart" features in "online malls," and obviously exist for no purpose other than to get customers either for existing offline businesses or to sell directly over the Internet.

Once you accept the fact that your ecommerce Web site's mission is to *sell*, and that the most effective way to *sell* is to *focus on selling*, the idea of providing news or entertainment on your *sales site* in order to lure visitors to it starts to look silly. Once you get focused this way, you can stop worrying about the gross number of visitors your site attracts, too. Raw popularity is not important for an ecommerce site. Sales volume is its one and only measure of success. A site that attracts one million visitors every day is going to run up big server and bandwidth bills, and if only a few hundred of those visitors spend $100 each, that site is a money-losing failure, while a site that gets only 1000 visitors per day, and gets three of those visitors to part with $100, can turn a modest profit if the goods or services it sells are priced correctly and the site itself is built and maintained on a tight budget.

Get to the Point Right Away

Since we're going to concentrate on selling, the first thing we want a potential customer to see on our site is our merchandise, just like a store window. We don't want to force potential customers to wade through a "welcome to our site" message of any kind, let alone a slow-loading animated one, before showing off our wares. Look at the color ad inserts in a Sunday newspaper. Their covers launch straight into their sales messages, usually with some sort of special offer or sale. If there is any institutional message on that insert's cover, it is usually stuck in one of the lower corners of the page, below plenty of "buy now" copy and product illustrations.

The only sites that need to display pictures of CEOs or VPs on their front pages are run by consulting or seminar companies that sell their corporate officers' expertise directly to clients. Retail-level purchasers looking for good deals on DVD players or toys to give to young relatives as gifts are more interested in the items they want to buy than in the corporate infrastructure behind the company selling them. A few words about that infrastructure and the people behind it should be on the site somewhere—that's what "about" pages are for—but should not be the first thing a potential customer sees.

A site section containing an "animated tour" of the company or its offerings, with a prominent link to that page on the site's main page, may not be a bad thing, but *forcing* customers to sit through an animated presentation as a condition of viewing products or services you offer is not going to increase sales. If you are selling software, the first thing a visitor to your site will want to know is what software you have for sale, an idea of its functions, and what kind of systems can use it. These are all necessary pieces of information for potential purchasers.

The NoteTab site's front page, shown in Figure 3–1, is a near-perfect online software marketing machine. It tells us what NoteTab does and what variations of it are available. We see a

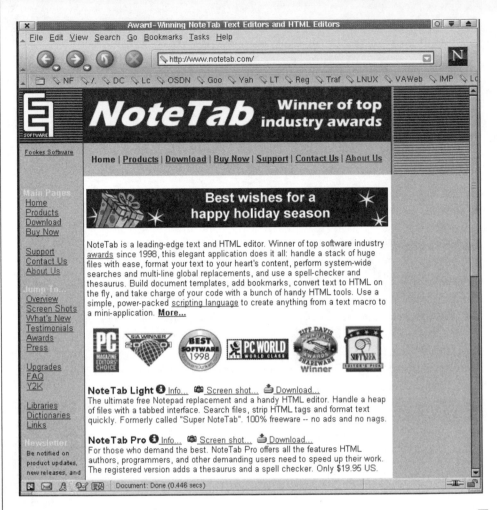

Figure 3–1   NoteTab home page.

series of award icons that tell us, in essence, "An awful lot of people who test software for a living say NoteTab is good stuff." We
have easy links to every bit of information we need to buy NoteTab
or, if we prefer, download a free "light" version to test before we
lay out money for either the "Pro" or "Standard" version. This site
has no splash page, and the only illustrations on it are small and
have few colors, so it loads rapidly on any Internet connection. It
uses no Javascript, Java, Flash, or anything else beyond simple
HTML, so it displays correctly in any popular browser running any
common operating system.

The NoteTab "About Us" page, shown in Figure 3–2, is not
thick with information, because this is a simple company with a

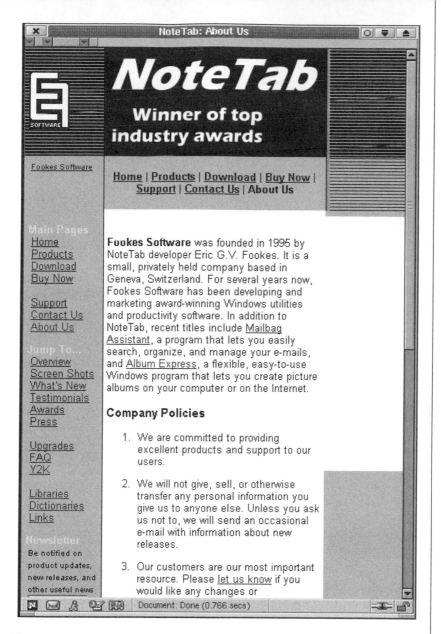

Figure 3–2   NoteTab "About Us" page.

small and simple product line. It is exactly as informative as it needs to be and no more. It tells us that NoteTab has been around since 1995, that it is produced by Fookes Software, a private company that was founded by Eric G.V. Fookes, and that the company has strict policies about customer privacy and satisfaction. We see links to several other Fookes software products, contact information, and, on the left side of the page, the same simple navigation links we saw on the home page—they are on every page on the site—that will take us instantly to any other piece of information about NoteTab that might help us decide to buy it.

The NoteTab site uses information layering well; we start with the basics on the home page, and if we're interested we can easily move to pages that go deeper into each program's features displayed as fast-loading text, with the option of slow-loading, but with more informative, full-page screenshots. We can learn as much or as little as we want about the three NoteTab versions, including price data, with only a few clicks, and we are never more than a single link away from the "Buy Now" page, where you have a choice of several methods of payment and product delivery (see Figure 3–3).

No one is going to call the NoteTab site a thing of beauty. From an artistic standpoint, "clunky" is probably the kindest single word we can use to describe it. But as a sales tool, it is totally effective and, because it is so simple and takes up so little server space and uses so little bandwidth to deliver, it is about as cost-effective as a Web site can get. The basic design hasn't changed in years, and the only copy on it that changes at all frequently is the "news" section on the home page, which carries nothing but news about NoteTab itself, not news about HTML editors in general or HTML developments.

Fookes Software doesn't handle its own order processing. This function is subcontracted. Since Fookes isn't handling credit cards, checks, or product delivery in-house, the company doesn't need to worry about keeping customer credit card numbers out of hackers' hands, setting up and maintaining a customer database or any of the other complicated details that must take place behind the happy face of an ecommerce Web site if it is going to run smoothly. All Fookes does is write software and market it through a Web site that probably took no more than a few days to make.

The market for NoteTab is easily defined, so promotion for the product is relatively simple; there are several dozen software listing sites that have substantial enough readerships to worry about, and NoteTab is prominently (and correctly) listed in all of them. And, of course, it is regularly and favorably reviewed, because it is an excellent piece of software, which probably is a bigger key to its success than the Web site. But all in all, this is a near-perfect example of how to sell a product efficiently over the Internet.

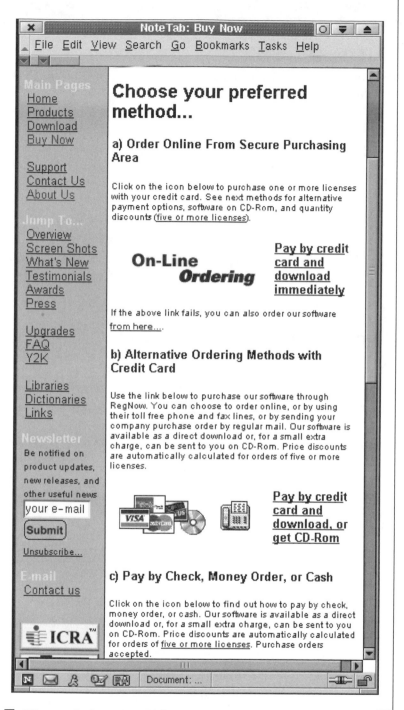

■ Figure 3–3   NoteTab "Buy Now" page, partial view.

Clear Product Descriptions Are Essential

Unless you are selling raw commodities to a well-defined market that is already familiar with their properties, you must provide clear descriptions of every product and treat every word on your site as sales copy. If your business is already established offline, that copy should be written in the same style as your printed sales material, either by the same people who write your print copy or by Web-specific writers who are in constant, close communication with your offline marketing staff. Style unity will keep customers who look at your Web site one minute and your printed material the next from getting confused, and one thing we never want is a customer who is confused about who we are and what we are selling.

Site Navigation for Ecommerce

The two most common methods of setting up a navigation scheme for an ecommerce site are product indexes and product grouping. A direct index that lists items by manufacturer and product number is the fastest navigation method for someone who *already knows what he or she wants to buy*, but it is nearly useless for someone who is browsing for something, like an inkjet printer, and may not know one model from another. This person is better off navigating through product groupings, where a number of similar products are displayed on one page and can easily be compared with each other. A third, less common method of indexing products is by brand name. This is not as useful to most customers as the other two, but it pleases suppliers, and this is a factor that should not be overlooked by any retail or wholesale merchant, especially since co-op advertising deals through which manufacturers pay for some or all of a wholesaler's or retailer's promotional efforts on behalf of their products are starting to become as common online as they are today in newspaper, broadcast, and direct mail advertising.

If you must pick just one navigation method, product grouping is probably the most natural. It also lends itself best to information layering. The accompanying illustrations, from *MexGrocer.com*, show how product grouping and information layering work together.

Figure 3–4 *MexGrocer.com* main page.

Figure 3–4 shows the *MexGrocer.com* main page, the same one we saw in Chapter One. It's simple, it's easy to understand, and it gets right to the point, putting featured products in front of you as soon as it starts to load. There is no introductory page to get in your way, and you instantly know what kind of goods *MexGrocer.com* sells.

Let's assume your immediate interest is salsa, either because you're from Mexico and are now living in a part of the world where authentic Mexican ingredients are hard to find or because you once traveled to Mexico, liked what you ate there, and want to duplicate it at home. You probably don't have a specific brand of salsa in mind; perhaps your only experience with Mexican food was eating in restaurants, and you are not familiar with different brands or you have heard only of a few highly-advertised ones that may not necessarily be the best ones out there. Your next step on *MexGrocer.com* is to click on the "Salsas" link on the left side of the main page.

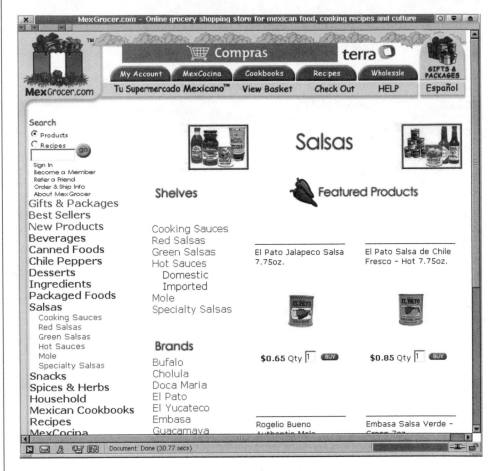

Figure 3–5 *MexGrocer.com* "Salsa" product page.

In Figure 3–5, you see some featured salsas and links to more, broken down by categories and brands. We don't know much about brands, but we know that we are going to use our salsa in our cooking, so we click on the "Cooking Sauces" link and go to a page that displays nothing but "Cooking Sauces."

We want to make enchiladas, and we like things mild instead of hot, so we click on "La Victoria Enchilada Sauce—Mild" (see Figure 3–6).

In Figure 3–7, the description looks good, and the price, $2.99 for a 28-ounce can, seems decent. Shall we buy it now? (We can almost taste those enchiladas!) But what about our diet? Shouldn't

Figure 3–6 *MexGrocer.com* "Cooking Sauces" category page.

we find out a little bit more about what we're talking about putting in our bodies? No problem. There's a "Nutrition Facts" link, and we click on it (see Figure 3–8).

Wow! No preservatives! That's good. Less than one gram of sugar per serving, which is within our acceptable range. Okay. We'll get some of this stuff. So we click the "go back" link (or use our browser's "back" button, and "add to basket," then look for some other items we might need to help us make a perfect, authentic Mexican dinner. But first, let's look at how *MexGrocer.com* used information layering to help us make our buying decision.

Figure 3–7 *MexGrocer.com* "La Victoria Enchilada Sauce" product page.

Information Layering Accommodates Almost All Shoppers

We looked at lots of product information, all the way down to nutrition specifications, before we bought our La Victoria enchilada sauce, but an experienced *MexGrocer.com* customer might not have wanted to see as much as we did. He or she might have clicked only as far as the page that displayed "Salsas," hit the "Buy" button next to the tiny (thumbnail) photo of the can of La Victoria Enchilada Sauce displayed there, then moved on to select other items from other areas of the site. Someone with no knowledge of

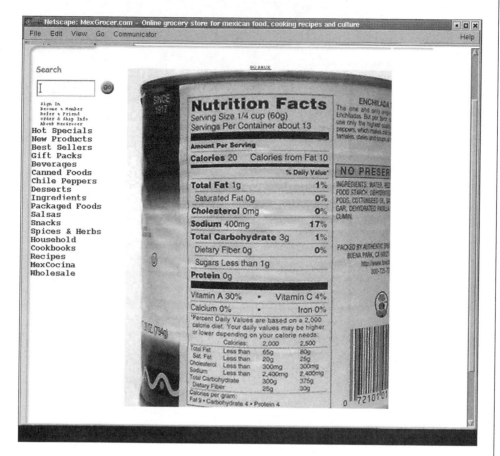

Figure 3–8 *MexGrocer.com* "Nutrition Facts" detail page.

enchilada sauces, but no worries about their diet, might have read the description of the product, looked briefly at the tempting enchiladas in the large photo of the can displayed on the product page, and bought from there without going to the "Nutrition Facts" page.

Experienced *MexGrocer.com* customers who have previously tried and enjoyed La Victoria Mild Enchilada Sauce have yet another alternative: They can use the little search form on the main page (it's also on most other pages on the site) to go directly to the product page, click "Buy," and repeat this process for 20 or 30 products, all in 10 minutes or less. (*MexGrocer.com* CEO Ignacio Hernandez says this is typical behavior for wholesale customers who put in monthly orders for multiple case lots instead of buying single units piecemeal.)

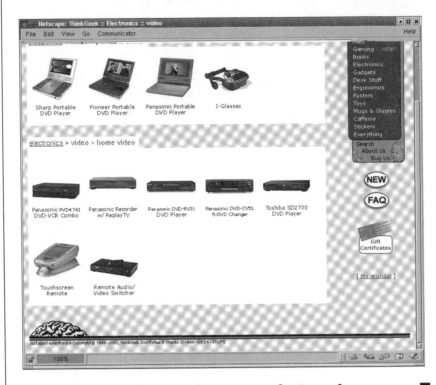

Figure 3–9 ThinkGeek "Home Video" product display.

MexGrocer.com has given us almost every conceivable navigation and selection option. All possible levels of customers, from first-time shopper to frequent wholesale buyer, are accommodated. The financial cost of making the site this easy to use for such a wide range of buyers was negligible. All it took was knowledge, whether conscious or unconscious, of information layering.

Information layering gives customers at all levels exactly as much buying data as they need without wasting anyone's download or attention time. The more complex the product you are selling, the more important this concept becomes. Consider a sophisticated touchscreen remote control device, as shown on the consumer electronics catalog page displayed here in Figure 3–9. This is a highly specialized product. Chances are, someone seeing this page for the first time didn't even know such a thing existed. There is no price shown for the item here; to get that information and learn more about this device, we click on the picture of the thing, which takes us to a page dedicated to this product.

Figure 3–10   ThinkGeek "Touchscreen Remote Control" product page.

In Figure 3–10, we see a feature list for this product, and the price. $479! Quite a chunk of change. You can get basic multi-unit remote controls for $20 or less in most discount stores. Obviously this is a specialty item that appeals to extreme gadget geeks, not the general public. Some may look at the feature list and small picture, say, "How cool!" and order one immediately. But a significant percentage may want to find out a little more before laying out close to $500, so there are links to additional information. Since part of the appeal of any "Look how cool I am" tech toy is visual, we have a "click for larger image" link (see Figure 3–11) that leads to a detailed picture of the device, along with several links to pictures of the remote's control screen for those who want to see more than one picture of the item before they consider buying it.

But the ultimate in geek product appeal is utility, not looks, so there's another link here, to a schematic diagram (see Figure 3–12) that explains all of this remote's many functions in pictorial form. Those who want this level of detail can get it with a click, and those who don't want it don't have to see it, same as with the nutritional

Figure 3–11   ThinkGeek "Touchscreen Remote Control—Big Picture" page.

information for the enchilada sauce. As is always the case with correctly-done information layering, the customer has a choice instead of having a vendor-selected set of information shoved down his or her throat.

Database-Driven vs. Static HTML Sites

A small site that features only a few products, like _NoteTab.com_, can easily be made and maintained using nothing but basic HTML code that almost anyone can teach himself or herself to write in a few days. These are "static" pages. If most site elements (logo, links, etc.) are going to be on all pages, they don't need to be rewritten "fresh" each time you change a page's content or add a new page. But when you get to the point where you are carrying

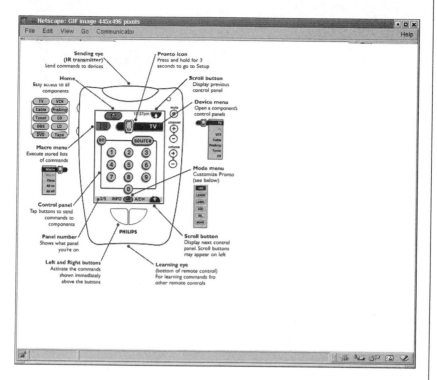

Figure 3–12   ThinkGeek "Touchscreen Remote Control—Schematic" page.

more than about 100 products, each of which requires an illustration, and each of which may be subject to frequent price changes, you will be better off using a database and creating dynamic pages instead of static ones.

When a user's browser calls for a page, and you're operating a Web site that runs on static HTML, the process is simple. Your server sends a single file that contains all the words and HTML code needed to recreate that page on the user's screen, plus a separate piece of code for each picture. Keep your HTML simple and the number (and size) of pictures down and each page will load quickly. Things at your end are simple, too. Since there aren't a lot of files involved with making up each page, your server computer doesn't need a very fast hard drive or much processing power. You don't necessarily even need a computer designed as a server to do this job, and you may even be able to avoid paying an outside provider to host your site. If you have (or know someone who has) enough technical know-how to install Linux and Apache, the most common software ingredients in a low-cost server installation, and you have a DSL Internet connection, you can serve thousands of pages daily from almost any old computer you have laying around.

Sites running "back-end" databases are more complicated. Instead of having each page stored as a single entity, dynamic sites (as these are called) assemble each page from parts, and put those parts into a pre-determined template every time a user's browser sends a page-request signal to your server. Instead of accessing a single HTML file and several graphics files in order to send a page, a database-driven site may access a separate file for each block of text displayed, plus a file for each graphic, plus the template file for the page, then send all of these files to the user, whose browser then uses them to construct the page. The more text blocks and pictures on a page, the longer all this takes. To compensate, we end up using expensive, specialized server hardware to get the same results we could have gotten serving static pages from a castoff home computer, and because your server and the customer's must talk back and forth more times for every page put out than is needed for a static site, this means more bandwidth gets used. Even if you use free Open Source software to run a dynamic site (and there is plenty of excellent free software available out there that can do this), increased hardware and bandwidth expenses mean you are going to spend a lot more money to run a dynamic site than to operate a static one.

So why bother?

Look at the *MexGrocer.com* screenshots again. The pictures and product descriptions you see may be used on many pages. A dynamic site like *MexGrocer.com* can produce a page that contains pictures of all products sold under a preferred brand name (Victoria), of all products in a given category (salsas), or of all products needed to make a particular dish (enchiladas). A dynamic site can give a user the option of viewing "all scanners under $150" or "all residential real estate listings in Wellington, New Zealand with asking prices between $50,000 and $120,000." A dynamic site gives users more information layering options than a static site. It is also easier to maintain in the clerical and content sense than a static site. On a static site, if you display a product on three different pages, and you discontinue that product or change its price, you must make those changes three times. On a dynamic site, you need to change a product's database entry only once, and it will be deleted (or added or modified) everywhere it could conceivably be displayed on your site.

Another advantage of a dynamic site is that it can draw information from an existing product or inventory database. The same text and illustrations can be used to generate both a print catalog and an online virtual catalog, which cuts expenses for both if they are either made by the same production crew or by offline and online marketing crews that work closely together. The next step in full utilization of a product database is to tie it to inventory and purchasing and to make it a true end-to-end ERP (Enterprise Resource Planning) tool that not only helps make sales, but also manages other aspects of your business including ordering, inventory, and future resource needs. Or take it from the other direction: If your company is already using an ERP or inventory control database of some sort, use that as the basis of your Web site. The cost of adding a few fields to an inventory database (like photos and customer-friendly product descriptions) so that it can become the basis of a catalog-style Web site is tiny compared with what you spent to set up the ERP database in the first place.

The problem with all of this database work, especially for small entrepreneurs, is that it is not cheap. Setting up and maintaining a workable, large-scale, database-driven ecommerce Web site is a full-time job for professionals. You may be able to hold costs down somewhat by hiring freelancers or an outside company to design and set up the site, and you may also be able to rely on outsiders to do most of its ongoing technical maintenance, but you will almost certainly want to have at least one in-house Web project manager to make sure everything works right—someone who spends a fair amount of his or her time simply calling up pages on the site to make sure that they all display correctly, and is responsible for making sure product descriptions, prices, and illustrations are always up to date. This person need not be a programmer, systems administrator, copywriter, or graphics designer, but should have at least some knowledge of what all of these people do and how to get them to work effectively.

How much of the work should be done in-house, versus farming it out, is one of those questions that must be answered case by case. If your company is large enough to have a sizable IT department anyway, you might as well keep the technical work in-house. If you already have graphics people on the payroll, training a few of them in Web design is probably a good investment, and you may find that some of the people working for you in art-related jobs are already doing at least some Web design on the side and will jump at the chance to do more of it.

A smaller company that relies on contractors or freelancers to handle computer work and graphics, may want to keep using contractors or freelancers—possibly the same ones it already uses for print graphics production—when moving onto the Web.

Businesses too small to have either their own in-house computer people or steady relationships with outside computer contractors or graphics designers should probably avoid making their own database-driven, dynamic Web sites as long as they can. A cleverly-designed static site can provide plenty of functionality at little cost, and while maintaining it can be somewhat tedious, that maintenance can be performed by properly-trained clerical workers who cost much less to employ than programmers or systems administrators. The point at which it becomes cost-effective to switch from a static site to a database-driven one is an individual business decision. The "over 100 products" rule is only a rough guide but, in general, switching too late is better than switching too soon. An ecommerce business that is so profitable that it needs upgrading is better than one with a sophisticated infrastructure behind it that is losing money because it has a complex, expensive Web site, but isn't attracting many customers.

The Myth of the Abandoned Shopping Cart

The shopping cart metaphor has become almost universal in ecommerce. A site user checks out products, then clicks on some sort of "buy this" link and goes on (hopefully) to select other products, adds them to his or her virtual cart, and finally goes through a checkout process at the end where he or she types in a shipping address and, at least for most consumer-level online purchases, credit card information. A common complaint, one about which many magazine and online articles have been written, is that ecommerce site users tend to abandon shopping carts at a frightful rate, generally estimated at between 60% and 80% by industry experts.

The reason for all those abandoned shopping carts is simple: The only way a customer can get a total price for a purchase, including shipping, from the vast majority of ecommerce sites is to make all of his or her product selections and go through the entire checkout procedure, right up to the point of typing in credit card information or clicking on a "finalize this purchase" button of some sort. Shipping charges can vary wildly from merchant to merchant, and on some products they are a large enough percentage of the total price that they can significantly influence a potential customer's buy/don't buy decision process. If a smart customer wants to check the total cost of a group of items, including shipping, from three different online merchants, by definition he or she is going to abandon two-thirds of the shopping carts used while choosing a vendor.

One thing to do about abandoned shopping carts is to ignore them. They aren't real shopping carts left in a real store's aisles where they inconvenience other shoppers, just digital fictions not worth a great deal of anguish. Another possibility is to make it easy for customers to save their shopping data on their own computers so they can look at the products they were thinking of purchasing at their leisure, then come back later and take up where they left off with a minimum of fuss. This feature would take a little thought, and a bit of programming, but would not be hard to implement.

A third alternative would be to abandon the shopping cart metaphor altogether. Surely someone as bright as you can come up with an interesting alternative, one that is as easily understood but not as tied to a physical allegory.

Tell Your Customers Who and Where You Are

No one likes to give money to strangers. This is why personal relationships are so important in so many sales-oriented fields, and why the expression, "Would you buy a used car from this man?" has become part of our lexicon. The implication here is that you would not buy a used car from someone you perceive as untrustworthy. It is important, when making an ecommerce Web site, to ask yourself at every step of the way, "Would I buy so much as a door knob from this company?"

There are certain very basic confidence-building ingredients that every ecommerce site should contain, but surprisingly few do:

- Full street address, including city, state or province, country, and postal code.
- Telephone and fax number.
- Hours of operation, including time zone.
- At least one picture of the company's physical place of business.
- Pictures (preferably) or at least brief biographies of the company's founders, principals, and key employees (on a separate "About Us" page; in keeping with the information layering concept, we want this information available, but do not want to ram it down the throat of every site visitor every time he or she visits our main page).

By including this information, we humanize our company in the eyes of our potential customers. It is no longer just a Web site run by a faceless company or individual, but is run by people.

If your company is large, you can impress potential customers with the breadth of resources it offers. If it is an old-line company, you can call upon your proud history to instill confidence. If you are going into a new venture, you can speak of how you need every customer and want to give great service so that you can grow. If you are a solo entrepreneur or just have a few co-workers, you can make a virtue of personalized service. If you have a tiny, cluttered shipping area, you can post a picture of it and boast about how you save your customers money by not investing in frills, and if you have an impressive warehouse or own retail stores, you can use photos of them to convey an impression of substance.

Whatever you do, be honest. Put the best face on who and what you are. Don't pretend that you and your partner, working from a garage in one of your homes, are really a multinational corporation with thousands of employees, and if your company is a multinational corporation with thousands of employees, don't pretend that you can offer service as personalized as two people working from a garage. Some potential customers are going to prefer dealing with a huge organization while others would rather deal with small entrepreneurs. Trying to pretend you are what you are not is not only dishonest, but also probably won't get you any more business than telling the truth.

Your "About Us" section is the one and only place on your site where you should display ego, and lots of it. If at all possible, have each employee whose face or bio is on your site write his or her own copy. Possibly a professional writer could do a slicker job, but then the individual personalities would be lost, and the whole point of this site section is to give the whole thing personality. It's a good idea to get a pro to look over your copy and correct obvious spelling and grammatical errors, and perhaps smooth out the statements a bit if they need it, but the essence of each person featured must come through.

There is no reason to confine bios to executives, either. Why not include at least a few customer service, shipping, and other front-line people? To your customers, if not to investors, they are the company.

Answer Your Email and Your Phone

There is no such thing as seamless ecommerce. Delivery trucks break down, orders get misplaced, computers crash, half the shipping department can be out with the flu. These problems are part of life, no matter how efficiently you run your business. Customers waiting for their orders want to know why their merchandise hasn't arrived on schedule, just as you would if you were in their shoes. They are going to call or email and ask what's going on. Your response or lack of response to those queries can easily determine whether or not the people sending them are going to remain your customers, and since it's almost always less expensive to hang on to customers you already have than to find new ones, you had better answer those inquiries as rapidly and honestly as you possibly can.

Email is probably the most common way for customers to ask about online orders they have placed. You *must* answer customer email as rapidly as possible, even if you stay late every night or authorize massive overtime to do it. Many of the horror stories that abounded during the first heavy ecommerce Christmas seasons in 1999 and 2000 had to do with lack of response to customer inquiries about misplaced or late orders. Many companies that had gone into the ecommerce business in 1998 or 1999 seemed to forget (or may never have known) that money would not roll in effortlessly through their Web sites, and that no matter how many times they repeated the mantra, "The Internet changes everything," ecommerce really didn't change anything except the way sales information is delivered to customers and the way that customers send orders to vendors. Freeways and expressways were still subject to traffic jams that made delivery trucks run late, and defective components were still a major annoyance to vendors and customers alike. And what changed least was human nature. Customers who didn't get deliveries on time or who got items delivered that didn't work or were damaged during shipping were as angry in the Internet era as they were back when goods were delivered by sailing ships and ox carts.

The only real difference between the Internet age and the pre-online world of postal mail order is that today's online customers expect to get answers to inquiries in hours, not in days or weeks.

But more insidious than email is the telephone. Email inquiries have at least some time slack to them. If a stack of them comes in all at once, and delays in responding to them are kept to eight hours or less, most customers will still be happy. In addition, with email, it is possible to come up with stock phrases that can be pasted into replies ("We're experiencing some delays because of a power outage to our warehouse that lasted from Monday evening through Thursday morning."). A human "Please bear with us" plea and a (true) explanation of (temporary) difficulties you face can go a long way toward mollifying upset customers if phrased correctly. Phone calls demand an entire different level of response speed. Modern humans don't like to be put on hold for more than a few minutes, and we don't like being forced to wade through voice mail menus. When we're calling to see why we haven't received our orders or why the merchandise we received didn't work, we are in no mood to wait. We want answers, and we want them now. When we hear, "If you know your party's extension, you may dial it at any time," we tend to curse under our breaths. It is not our job, we figure, to memorize your phone system. We have a problem, and we want a live human to pick up the phone and take care of it.

If you buy an item from an in-person vendor, you have the option of taking it back to the store if it doesn't work right. If there is a line at the customer service counter, you can see how long that line is and watch it inch along. There is a feeling of progress. Waiting on the telephone hold does not provide this kind of visual contact. There is no chance to talk to the person in front of or behind you in line. There is nothing to look at but a lonely telephone. This is not good service. You will not stand for it more than once if any other company, online or not, provides the same goods or services, and neither will your customers, with one situational exception: If your Web site has made it clear, right from the start,

that your business is tiny, run by only a few people, you can probably get away with taking messages and returning calls as long as
you make those callbacks promptly, and your "We're not here"
message has an actual name on it, along the lines of, "Hi, this is
Frank at (company name). Please leave a message and we'll call
you back within (number of hours)." A large business cannot get
away with this. Customers will, justifiably, mutter, "With all their
money, they can't afford to have anyone answer the phone?"

Too many Internet entrepreneurs fail to factor in the cost of
providing rapid email and telephone customer service, which can
be a substantial expense at all times, and can hit alarming peaks if
you run into a series of product defects or delivery problems. You
must be prepared to move a significant percentage of your personnel to customer service, almost immediately, if you experience
a higher number of complaints than usual. When your only contact
with your customers is through the Internet or by phone, you must
make those contacts as pleasant as possible if you are going to build
a long-term Internet business.

Do You Really Need Ecommerce?

This question is rarely asked, especially by people who are trying
to sell you Web design, site hosting, or other Internet services, but
it is a valid one. Many businesses are better off with a simple
brochure-style online presence than with a full-featured, interactive Web site. Building a simple business promotion site is easier
and less costly than making and maintaining one that has features
like shopping carts, customer feedback forms, and database-gen-
erated catalog pages.

Before you decide to jump into ecommerce, you should think
long and hard about whether it is right for you and your business.
A business promo site is not the same as an ecommerce site.
Indeed, the difference between the two is great enough to warrant
an entirely separate chapter about using the Internet to promote
an offline business. Small business owners, especially, should read
Chapter 4 before they consider moving into ecommerce.

Promotional Web Sites for Offline Businesses

Hardly anyone talks seriously about how to make promotional Web sites for offline businesses. Ecommerce gets plenty of attention, but there are many businesses that can't use the Internet directly as a sales medium.

There is, as yet, no way a hairdresser can do a permanent wave online; customers still need to go to the shop in person to get their hair done. Auto mechanics and building contractors still need to wield physical tools to do their jobs. Hospitals get more computerized and Net-savvy every year, but you still can't get thoracic surgery delivered to your door by going to a Web site, clicking on a "cure my disease" link, and typing in your credit card number.

But hospitals, auto mechanics, hairdressers, building contractors, law firms, real estate brokers, restaurant owners, and many others whose products or services require in-person contact can and do use the Internet as an effective business promotion tool.

The primary difference between an ecommerce Web site and a promotional site for an offline business is that the promotional site is designed to generate sales leads, not sales. The ecommerce site needs to supply every bit of information a prospect needs to make a "buy" decision—and the tools to carry it out, then and there, through an online form—while the promotional site needs to offer only enough information to generate a phone, postal mail, email, or walk-in sales inquiry.

The amount of information needed to produce that inquiry depends on your individual business and the market it serves. No book can give you a stock formula that will fit all situations. The old rule, "The more you tell, the more you sell," certainly applies, as long as you use information layering so that each individual site visitor isn't forced to wade through pages full of information which he or she doesn't need to get to the information which he or she does need.

The more your site tells potential customers about your products or services, and about your business in general, the less qualifying you will have to do when they contact you. The perfect customer, in many ways, is one who already knows what he or she wants, walks in the door, and buys it without a great deal of conversation. But at the same time, telling so much on your Web site that a customer fixates on one item may kill your chance to offer additional products or services or to show other products if the customer doesn't like the first one after seeing it in person.

As a general rule, the first promotional Web site you put up should err on the side of simplicity. Just as it is most prudent to start with a small showroom and expand later if you get enough business to justify it, and a small, busy restaurant is more likely to make money than a large one that is never full, it is best to start with the simplest possible site for your business and expand it gradually.

Location, Location, Location

The single most important piece of information on a local business's Web site is its address, including city or town, state or province, country, and Zip or postal code. This needs to be on every page, easily readable by anyone who finds that page through a search engine or personal referral. The Web is truly World Wide, and search technology is imperfect. A potential client trying to find a real estate agent in Baltimore, County Cork, Ireland, is also going to get search engine referrals to agents in Baltimore, Maryland, USA, and probably to many agents in places that don't have "Baltimore" in their names.

Realizing that the Web is truly World Wide seems to be the hard-

Like Everything Else, Simplicity Has Its Limits

The fictitious business promotion site shown in Figure 4–1 is an example of usability taken to an unhealthy extreme. An all-text page like this will load in the blink of an eye over even the slowest modem connection, and it is certainly easy to navigate; all the links are underlined, and all underlined words are links, in accordance with the most basic usability rules.

But if you came across a page that looked like this while searching the Web for (yes, I'm making this up) Rotary Relinearizing Equipment, would you give this site a second glance?

Probably not.

Any quality, including simplicity, can be taken too far.

Figure 4–1   The world's simplest promotional Web site.

est mindset change for local businesses that are just moving onto the Internet. When writing a flier to be hand-distributed in the immediate neighborhood, an ad for placement in a local newspaper, a TV spot that is going to run only on local stations, or a local telephone directory listing or ad, there is no need to say what country you're in, or, in most cases, what state or province. You can safely assume that nearly 100% of a local ad's readership is going to be located near your business, and potential customers will automatically assume your business is local to them as well. This is, of course, a false assumption on the Internet. No one knows where you are unless you explicitly tell them, and you must give them your full telephone number too, including area or region code and, if appropriate for your business, the country code as well, because one of the great reasons Web users search for local businesses is that they are moving or traveling to a place for which they don't have local print directories handy, and are trying to arrange for essential services at their new location before they leave the old one.

Are You Going to Answer Email?

This is a legitimate question. Not every business is set up to respond to a constant barrage of email inquiries within 24 hours, and in a world that moves at "Internet speed," an email that does not generate a reply within 24 hours might as well not be answered at all. If you are not really, for sure, always going to answer email rapidly, you may be better off either leaving your email address off the site or inserting this line: "Please allow up to three days for an email response; if you have an immediate request, our telephone lines are open from [time] to [time], [time zone]." You may also want to consider the wisdom of publishing a toll-free phone number on your Web site, since it is a service that can easily be abused by out-of-towners who are curious about your business but are not likely to become customers. If a significant part of your trade does not come from outside of your area already or you are in a business where markups are thin, you are probably better off showing only your local phone number on the Internet.

The idea of downplaying email as a means of corporate communication on a Web site may seem illogical to ardent Net users, but it is easy to get into a mental state that says, "If it's not on the Internet it doesn't exist." Even in the most connected countries, places like the United States, Finland, and Germany, this is not true. There are plenty of people, possibly a majority of those who have Net connections, who use the Internet as a necessary tool, not as an all-day, every-day source of commercial and personal interaction. Most of the people who make Web sites and sell Web services are in the "Internet is life, and life is Internet" crowd, and may often be heard talking about "Real Life" or "The Big Blue Room" (outdoors) as something they experience only now and then when they get eyestrain from too many hours looking at their biggest-on-the market computer monitors.

But unless you are selling Internet-specific products or services, most of your prospective customers probably do not fit into this mold. They are people who have lives: They use services like dry cleaning, they eat out in restaurants, hire limousines, buy airline tickets, go to night clubs, send greeting cards, need lawyers now and then, enjoy a massage, worry about maintaining their automobiles, go to concerts, buy houses, have babies who then need to be fed and clothed, and, in general, do things besides hang out online. They may not even enjoy sending or receiving email, and may use the Internet only as a glorified shopping catalog. If you provide any of the products or services listed above, people who do not live online are more likely to spend money with you than those who do, and they are used to either calling stores and service providers by phone or walking into your place of business and looking at your merchandise or discussing your services in person.

In other words, people who devote their lives to the World Wide Web may not always be the best source of advice about building a Web site that has, as its only purpose, facilitating business that takes place offline. So, no matter what the heavy-duty Web heads say, if your business is not set up to deal with email, and you are comfortable with the way you run things now, don't encourage email. Believe it or not, you can get plenty of business from a promotional Web site without email.

Start Small, then Grow

A small business's first Web site can be so simple that a skilled Web designer can build it in an hour or less—probably after spending several hours telling you why you need more features than you really need at the beginning. Here are the necessary ingredients:

- Business name, address, and telephone number.
- Catchy description of products and services offered.
- Several paragraphs of sales copy that give customers quantifiable reasons why they should patronize your business instead of a competitor's.

- Several pictures of the physical facility, not totally devoid of life, but with employees and, hopefully, customers, in at least some of the shots.

This kind of Web site can be put together rapidly and cheaply, never needs to be revised unless you change your products or services, or move or change your telephone number, and can be hosted by any one of thousands of ISPs or Web hosting services for as little as $10 per month, which is less than a bold-faced listing costs in many local telephone directories. How much business it will bring in depends on local conditions, how well the site is placed in search engines, and the general level of demand for the products or services you provide.

We are talking minimum effort here, a glorified brochure that costs next to nothing to distribute—one that can contain color pictures at no extra cost and that has no print-style text length restrictions. A humble site, perhaps, but there is nothing wrong with that. More information can be added later. It is better to start small and grow than to enter with a bang and later retreat with a whimper.

Make Sure You Own Your Name

The one thing that is a must, from the very beginning, is your own domain name. One that reads *yourname.hostname.com* is not yours. It belongs to the Web hosting service. If they change their policies or prices and you want to leave them, you lose your online identity. A domain name of your own costs less than $20 per year. Yes, the simplest and shortest ones (*car.com*, for example) are already taken, but with a little imagination you will easily find one that works for your business, possibly as easily as testing your own company name, perhaps combined with your location, at *www.internic.net/whois.html*, the largest domain name registrar's lookup page. Sooner or later, if you try enough names, you will come across one that fits your business.

Remember, though, that a domain name you think is catchy may not please your customers as much as it pleases you. What they want and need is something easy to remember that directly relates to your business, not something cute and frothy. It is always better to go with something like AlsArtGallery (assuming your name is Al

Never Forget to Pay Your Domain Name Bill!

On December 25, 1999, Microsoft Network's Hotmail service starting giving users error messages like "unable to locate host" or "no such domain." Since Hotmail had tens of millions of users, this caused a certain amount of panic among Windows and Microsoft Network (MSN) users who relied on Hotmail for their online communications.

The problem turned out to be with Microsoft's "Passport" authentication service, which was (and still is) an integral part of Hotmail, MSN, and now, Microsoft's heavily promoted .NET services, which will, according to Microsoft, revolutionize the way we use both computers and the Internet. To use any of these services your identity must first be confirmed through Passport.

The 1999 Christmas "Passport failure" occurred because Microsoft had forgotten to pay the bill for Passport's domain name, so the big root servers at the heart of the Internet would not resolve (translate) browser requests for "*Passport.com*" into the numerical address (some-thing like "207.68.179.63") computers know it by. Because of this, Passport was invisible to the world. And because *Passport.com* disappeared, many Microsoft services, not just Hotmail, stopped working.

Every business, big or small, must pay its domain name bills if it wants its site to show up. Microsoft doesn't get an exception, and neither do you.

The funny part of the Passport story is that the person who put *Passport.com* back on line did not work for Microsoft. Michael Chaney, a Linux consultant in Nashville, Tennessee, used his MasterCard to pay the outstanding bill to Network Solutions, Microsoft's domain registrar, through their online payment form. The bill was $35.

Microsoft later sent Chaney a check for $500, a rather small amount considering that Microsoft's failure to pay $35 was probably costing the company hundreds of thousands of dollars per hour even on Christmas Day, which is traditionally one of the lowest Internet traffic days.

What if This Had Happened to Your Business?

Imagine a customer or potential customer going to your site and finding it gone. He or she emails you, but since corporate email addresses are usually tied to the corporate domain name, the mail bounces back as undeliverable. As far as that customer is concerned, you have gone out of business unless your company is as big and well-known as Microsoft or a kind, Chaney-like customer comes to your rescue.

People talk about owning domain names, but in reality they are rented. No matter what else you do or don't do on the Internet, you must pay that domain name rent on time, every time.

and you run an art gallery) than CoolArtz, because CoolArtz does not help drum your business's name into the heads of potential customers, and this is (hopefully) the main reason you are making a promotional Web site in the first place. (Of course, if you come up with a domain name you really love, you can always change your business name to match it. You wouldn't be the first person to do this, either.)

Adding Prices and Other Content

A never-changing site takes no work, once it is online, besides making payments for your domain name and hosting service when they are due, usually once a year.

Let's assume that your initial Web site draws enough business to be worth its keep. The next step is obviously to add content to it that may change from time to time. The most obvious question that your potential customers are likely to ask is, "How much does it cost?"

Now you get into the question of how much to tell them. This is an individual business decision, one you must base on your industry, your location, and the nature of the competition you face. And the second you start adding prices to your Web site, you suddenly must commit to keeping it up to date. No business needs customers complaining that an advertised price is incorrect. You may put a disclaimer on your site saying that prices should be confirmed before purchase or that you are not responsible for errors in prices shown on the World Wide Web, but all this will do is help keep you out of legal hot water. Inaccurate pricing on your Web site will still damage your reputation. Prices shown on your site, just like prices in a newspaper ad, must be the real prices you charge for real goods and services.

Changing a few lines on a Web site is not hard. You or one of your co-workers can easily learn to do it, either through one of the many basic HTML classes offered online or through local adult learning centers and community colleges almost everywhere in the world, or by simply buying a book or two and practicing on a fake site you set up that is not visible to the public. The elements of HTML code are simple, and the popular file transfer protocol (ftp) method of uploading content to a Web server is handled by easily-obtained, free or low-cost programs that usually take less than an hour of practice to master.

Simple Web site updating is also easy to farm out. It doesn't take design or programming skills. It's really nothing but a specialized form of clerical work, easily performed by almost anyone who has made a hand-coded personal Web site or two. Who prepares the actual site copy is up to you, and depends on your personnel resources. One advantage the Web has over print is that mistakes are easy and inexpensive to rectify after publication. If you find a typo after you have added new or updated material to your site, it is the work of moments to correct it. This doesn't mean you should allow sloppy wording to get by you. Rather, it means that you or your site maintenance person should be able to make the copy on your Web site better—and keep it more timely— than the copy in your printed materials.

Just as with any other kind of Web site, the basic design and architecture of a promotional site need to be carefully thought out in advance, and for best results the concept of information layering should be applied just as strictly to a site with three or four simple pages as to one with 500 pages.

Avoid Web Obsession

This is a danger that is rarely discussed, but is clear and present for any businessperson who puts up a Web site for the first time. The Web is addictive, not only for users but also for site owners. The ease with which a Web site can be changed has seduced many site owners into constant experimentation, even daily changes that produce little or no return in the form of increased business. The expression, "If it ain't broke, don't fix it" applies to Web sites as much as to anything else in life (or in business).

There is nothing inherently wrong with wanting to improve your Web site, but letting that part of your business occupy too much of your attention will inevitably take your mind away from other areas that need it.

One reason many executives probably make too-frequent changes to their sites is boredom. It is easy to forget that while you may look at your site every day (or, if you are truly obsessed with it, many times daily), even your most devoted customers see it only once in a while, and new customers and prospects have never seen it before, so what is old hat to you is new to them. There's an important lesson here:

Put Yourself in Your Customer's Shoes

This is another one of those classic business homilies that applies as much on the Internet as it does anywhere else. You can't really do it, of course, because you know too much about your business to view it with fresh eyes. Your Web site is there for people who know nothing (or at least very little) about your business. You put it up to enlighten them, not (hopefully) as an ego-gratification device. At the same time, self-promotion, in the business sense, is its primary purpose. You probably will not be able to strike an appropriate balance on your own. You need help.

If you have a large, well-funded business there are many companies that run focus group studies to help you get a customer's eye view of your operation, and many of them will as happily apply their methods and expertise to a proposed Web site as they will to any other aspect of your company—for a fee, naturally.

A less expensive alternative is to go first to co-workers, then to friends and relatives, and ask them to judge your site. Ideally, to duplicate the typical customer experience as closely as possible, they should look at your site on their own home or office computers, using their preferred operating systems and Web browsers. Then you'll find that, no matter how firmly you ask for honesty, even brutal honesty, a lot of your informal focus group friends are just going to say, "Looks fine to me."

This is when you need to start asking direct questions.

Some good questions to ask follow:

(all prefaced with, "From information on our Web site, did you learn...")

- Our business name?
- Where we are located?
- Exactly what products/services we offer?
- Who runs the place?
- How to contact us?
- What we look like (both facility and people)?
- When we're open?
- Why you should buy from us instead of someone else?

Note that these questions follow the old journalistic "Who, what, when, where, why, and how" pattern. This is a good pattern for a business brochure, either online or print, too, because these are the basic bits of knowledge a customer needs in order to find a vendor that fits his or her needs. Everything else on your site is spin, puffery, and cuteness that can be classified under the "Why you should buy from us" category. It's fine to have lots of it, if that's your business style, but you must not let it obscure the basic stuff.

But these are really just "loosening up" questions. You've used them to establish a dialog beyond the "Looks fine to me" level. Now you can launch a more substantive inquiry. Some examples follow:

- How long did our main page take to load? Did it take longer than you would have liked?
- Were the pictures too big? Too small? Just right?
- Did we tell you enough about our business? Should we have told you more? If so, what? Should we have told you less? Did our text ramble too much? Should it be shortened?
- Did we put information in the right order? How could we reorder our site layout and content to make it easier to use?
- How about the colors? Was our text easy to read? Could you tell hyperlinks from ordinary text without any problem?

You can certainly think of many additional questions specific to your business. Ask them. Ask them of friends, relatives, customers, and anyone else you know. Ask 10, 20, even 100 people. Listen closely to their answers and write them down. And then, steel yourself and get ready for the hardest part of this whole process:

Giving Your Web Site Visitors What They Want

The reason you do a lot of thinking before you make a Web site, and quiz others about it after you put it up, is to make your site as useful and business-inducing as possible, not for yourself or your co-workers, but for current and potential customers. You may be a business genius and an expert in your field, but your customers know more about what they need from your Web site than you do. They are the experts here, the "outside consultants" you have called on for advice.

It is disheartening when people you trust kick your carefully planned Web site around and tell you all the things you did wrong, but there is only one sane response: Implement the suggestions you got.

When a hired Web designer tells you his or her work is "the latest thing" or "is made with the customer in mind," and the lay people whose opinions you solicited are either neutral toward the design or don't like it at all, the Web designer is wrong and the ordinary people are right. You can hire the world's best usability consultant to help you make a brilliant Web site, but if the first response your friends and customers have to it is, "Ewww... that's ugly," you must listen to your friends and customers, not to your hired consultant, no matter how much you paid for his or her advice.

In the end, the only true measure of a promotional Web site's quality is the amount of business it brings in. Artistic merit is not a major concern in and of itself. Beauty is good, certainly, but only as a tool to attract customers. Usability is an excellent goal, too, but if you sacrifice esthetics to easy navigation and as a result of that decision you make a site that people don't enjoy seeing on their monitors, you have gone too far in the other direction.

The best judges of where the compromise line between artistic merit and usability should be drawn are the people who are going to view and use your site. They will not all agree with each other, but if you ask enough friends, co-workers, relatives, and customers for their opinions, a rough consensus will eventually emerge, and that consensus must be your guide.

You can augment the effectiveness of your focus group's input by giving them a number of different versions of your Web site to look at, assuming you have time and budget to make multiple layouts. This tends to produce more concrete and easily quantifiable advice than "Do you like this? If not, why not?" questioning about a single site design.

Think of the process of asking people for their opinions about two or three or ten different site versions as similar to an optometrist's "Is 'A' clearer than 'B'?" method of determining eyeglass prescription strengths, and use the same methods that an optometrist does, and you will end up with a Web site likely to please most of the people who see it most of the time, and that's about as good as you are going to get, considering that both esthetic and usability qualities are at least in part a matter of individual taste.

The Last Word: Stick to Business

A Web site meant to promote your business should do just that. Nothing else. If you want to have a personal Web page that tells the world how much you love your dogs, cats, or children, that's fine. Put one up, but *not* on your business site.

Want to share your political or religious philosophy with the world? Great. But set up a separate site to do it instead of adding religious or political pages or links to your business site—unless you make your living from religion or politics.

You should also avoid free Web hosting deals that put banner ads for other businesses on *your* site. It is better to lay out a few bucks every month to make sure your site boosts no one's business but yours.

The Web site that promotes your business has just one purpose: to bring in customers. Every single pixel on it must be dedicated to that goal.

News and Discussion Web Sites

Most of the major print publishers and broadcasters that went online in the 1990s have since scaled back their Internet activities because they haven't figured out how to make them profitable. If you think you can make money with a news Web site, you're saying, in effect, "I know more about producing news online than the people who run some of the world's biggest newspaper chains and broadcast networks."

Are you really that smart? Or have many of the big media companies that have tried to move online gone about it wrong? The answer to both questions just may be "Yes."

But don't kid yourself. Running an online news site—and making money at it—is one hell of a task, especially if you expect all or most of your revenue to come from banner advertising.

What about discussions and other reader-generated content? If you can get readers to send in stories (or links to stories published elsewhere) that generate hundreds of pages of discussion, shouldn't it be easy to make money, since all your content is free? Not exactly. Very few discussion sites earn a profit. Most are losers—at least in the financial sense.

The Free User-Generated Content Myth

The name millions of Web users know me by is "Roblimo," my nom-de-net on Slashdot (*www.slashdot.org*), a site started in 1997 by Rob "CmdrTaco" Malda, then a student at Hope College in Holland, Michigan. The site was a hobby at first. Rob and his friend Jeff "Hemos" Bates and a few others posted little stories and observations about technology, science, and computer software (especially Linux), and readers posted responses.

While Rob was busily starting Slashdot, I was freelancing for Netly News (part of Time Life's now-dead *Pathfinder* site) and assorted print publications, and operating a small but profitable limousine service. I enjoyed Slashdot thoroughly; not only were Taco's and Hemos' and their friends' articles fun to read, but they often made excellent points, and readers' posts added to those articles often made even better ones.

There was a pleasant, clubby feel to Slashdot in the early days. You could say almost anything, and almost anyone could say almost anything back. There was a little vituperation at times, but it was generally a good-hearted group.

Slashdot has drawn criticism for its poor English usage from the beginning, but I never minded Rob's loose—I prefer to call it "unique"—approach to spelling and grammar. If anything, I felt, it encouraged posts by others, especially programmers and technologists who were experts in their fields but not confident of their writing skills. The site's motto was (and still is) "News for Nerds. Stuff that matters," not "Stories and links posted only after careful proofreading by professional editors."

Fast-forward to early 1999. I'm writing and editing full-time for a small online publisher called Andover News Network that is running on venture capital and dreaming of an IPO. Taco and Hemos have graduated from college and are trying to make a full-time go of Slashdot. They're up to half a million pageviews a day, and they are overwhelmed by the sheer amount of work it takes to run the site. Linux use has exploded, and Linux news is now a large proportion of Slashdot's content. Linux companies are offering to buy Slashdot for ever more foolish amounts of cash and stock as both the general dot-com investment frenzy and the "Get rich from Linux" investment fads near their peaks.

For various reasons, including a contract that guarantees them nearly absolute editorial freedom, Rob and Jeff take Andover's offer, even though it is not as high as others they have gotten. Andover selects me as the editorial overseer of Slashdot and the Linux software index site freshmeat (*www.freshmeat.net*) which they also bought in mid-1999.

I was already more familiar with Slashdot than most; I had User ID #357 out of over 100,000 registered users (a number that grew to over 600,000 by the end of 2001, and is still growing). I was a regular, well-known participant in Slashdot discussions, and many stories I had written elsewhere had been linked to by Slashdot and dissected in some of those discussions. But I was not fully prepared for the overwhelming amount of work it took to make Slashdot run, seemingly without effort, day after day.

Evaluating Reader Submissions Takes Time

The first morning I actively worked on Slashdot, I found that almost 100 stories had been submitted overnight. By the time I had sorted through all of them, looking for the five or ten we might want to post to start the day, I easily could have written a full day's worth of Slashdot stories (generally about 15) on my own, and had the rest of the day to myself. I knew that this would have destroyed Slashdot, which is what it is because it is almost entirely reader-driven. But that first Slashdot submissions bin experience drove home something every Web publisher who wants to save money by replacing professionally-written material with reader-generated content must realize: The amount of time and effort it takes to find usable submissions in what amounts to a huge, ever-changing daily slush pile easily exceeds the amount of time it takes an experienced writer to produce the same amount of material from scratch.

Then there are the Slashdot reader comments. They are "free content" in an immediate sense, but in the long run they are not. A reader types his or her thoughts into an online form (or pastes copy written in a text editor into the form), touches a "submit" button, and the comment appears almost instantly. Content from heaven! Except that some of this "free content" may be full of obscenities; or contain other people's copyrighted material; or contain libelous statements or material that can otherwise cause trouble, including the kind of trouble that leads to high legal bills. Plus, in a reworking of Gresham's Law, "Bad money drives out good," about the debasement of currencies, a site full of *dreck* comments drives off readers who might have posted level-headed, intelligent ones.

At the same time, keeping posting fast and easy, and allowing anonymous posts, often gives Slashdot important reader-generated material found nowhere else. The balance between free speech and repelling readers (and attracting lawyers) can be thin and hard to define. Rob Malda's solution was to devise a system that would allow readers to moderate each other's comments, but would not allow a reader to both post and moderate in the same discussion. This worked up to a point, but around the time Slashdot started to get an average of one million daily pageviews, the system started breaking down because some readers decided to post comments that had no other purpose than to gain them moderation points, or "Slashdot karma," which defeated the original purpose of moderation.

Posts were rated on a scale of −1 to +5, and the default "moderation level" at which readers saw Slashdot discussions was +1. This made the worst posts invisible to someone who casually looked at Slashdot for the first time, although registered readers were free to change their normal viewing level either upwards so they saw only posts rated at +2 or +3 or higher, or downwards, right down to −1, so they could read everything, no matter how bad. And then came moderation system abusers who set up numerous Slashdot "identities" so they could post with one identity and moderate with another, and controls had to be instituted to keep *them* in check. Other Slashdot abusers wrote little software routines whose sole purpose was submitting obscene or useless material over and over, several times a minute, and more software had to be written to protect against them. It became a constant battle, one that has not ended and shows no sign that it is going to end as long as Slashdot exists. We simply accept the fact that there are thousands of Slashdot users who seem to think of the site as an online game rather than as a news and discussion system. Some of them even have sites and email groups set up where they talk about *nothing* but "trolling" Slashdot in one way or another.

"Thousands of Slashdot trolls" sounds like a lot, but Slashdot gets around one million pageviews on its slowest days, and over two million on its busiest ones. The abusers are only a tiny percentage of the total Slashdot population.

The problem with this whole game is that Slashdot's programmers are outnumbered and are constantly playing catch up. No sooner do they eliminate one loophole, such as writing a script that prevents some of the more prurient users from posting pornographic "art," than another user comes up with a new way to subvert the scheme. That problem gets solved, then another one comes up. This race has been going on, at an increasing pace, since Slashdot broke out of its original little club-like niche and started attracting a mass audience. More readers will only make the problem worse.

Slashdot's comment handling, even without defenses against unruly posters, takes hardware and software far more complex than you need to put up professionally-generated content on a fixed schedule. Slashdot's database has new entries written to it many thousands of times each day, and at the same time, thousands of users are accessing the site simply to read it. Comments don't come in, and pages aren't sent out, at an even hourly rate. There are peak load times when up to 100,000 users may try to access the site at almost exactly the same moment, while 1000 or more are simultaneously posting comments. This takes dozens of

server computers to handle, and the load balancing that makes them work together smoothly (at least most of the time) takes nearly constant human babysitting.

None of this would happen on a small discussion site that got only a few thousand visitors and a dozen posts per day, but that small site couldn't survive on ad revenue. You need a *minimum* of 50,000 daily pageviews to make any kind of profit from a discussion site, and from there on up you are going to discover that discussion sites don't scale as profitably as straight-up news sites. A story you write (or pay to have written), once posted, needs only to be served and sent out. The more people who read it the better, because the additional technical cost for each additional reader, once the story is written and saved to your server, is negligible, while the technical cost of hosting discussions goes up as your audience increases, not quite in a linear fashion but close enough to it that you will not see profit margins increase with additional readership nearly as fast as you will with content which you generate yourself.

Don't Forget the Lawyers

Professional journalists are usually keenly aware of legal issues. They are supposed to know how to "source" a story correctly; to take careful notes or make tape recordings of interviews so subjects can't later claim they were misquoted; to avoid copyright infringement or plagiarism, and generally avoid getting sued for petty reasons.

Volunteer posters have no such constraints. If you allow open posting on your site, you will inevitably attract comments that irritate someone who has an attorney on retainer, and when that happens, you had better have one of your own.

All meaningful legal complaints we have had at OSDN have been over reader contributions, and most of them originate on Slashdot. The most common problem is copyright infringement. We have had readers post everything from articles that belong to other online publishers, to pieces of the Church of Scientology's fiercely-defended "scriptures," to program code claimed by Microsoft Corporation.

I assure you, from personal experience, that hosting open discussions online can create more legal headaches than almost anything else you can do on the Internet.

Do you still want to run a discussion site, or have I talked you out of it?

The Economic Realities of Online Advertising

From 1994 to 2000, ad banner placement rates as high as $80 per 1000 pairs of eyeballs which saw each page that ad was on (called "pageviews" in the trade) were common. The theory (at the time) was that Internet users were more "engaged" than users of other media; that because of the Net's interactivity, ads on Web sites had a higher impact than TV spots or print ads. Another attraction of Web advertising was demographics; most early Web users were young, male, and prosperous, and by definition were early adopters, more open to new services and products than the general population. But what did they adopt early? Obviously, they bought computer hardware and software, Internet services, and other related items. But there was never any hard evidence that Internet users were more likely to buy consumer products as a result of Internet advertising than if they saw ads in other media touting them, so Internet ads did not appeal to packaged goods companies, like Proctor & Gamble or Lever Brothers, that are typically among the most prolific TV advertisers in the United States.

At $80 per thousand pageviews at the top end, 1990s Internet advertising was at least 10 times as expensive as prime-time TV. This might have been okay for companies in the computer industry, especially for ads on "geek" sites populated almost entirely by their most likely customers, but it certainly wasn't Anheuser-Busch's (or Lipton's) cup of tea. Perhaps one reason AOL has always been more successful than most at selling online ads is that it has tended to price well under the "dream" prices seen on other major online publishers' rate cards, with $5 to $15 CPM (cost per thousand pageviews) on many of the network's services in 1997, and as low as $2 CPM for some of its offerings after the "advertising meltdown" in 2001.

At $80 CPM—or even at a more common $40 to $50 CPM after haggling down from posted prices—a small solo entrepreneur could earn a decent living from 10,000 loyal readers who each viewed 10 pages on his or her site every week, or 100,000 total pageviews, which translated into $5,000 per week of gross income at $50 CPM, and $8,000 at $80 CPM. If you figure $2,000 per month for server and bandwidth expenses—the online equivalent of printing costs—and give half of the remainder to freelancers or a couple of salaried assistants, then online news looks like a lucrative business.

Now try to run that same site, with the same 100,000 weekly pageviews, on an income of $2 CPM. Suddenly gross income is $200 per week. Server and bandwidth charges may have dropped to $1,000 per month because the Web hosting business got more competitive between 1997 and 2001, but the site is still in the red.

By 2001, even targeted tech-news sites were having trouble getting more than $10 CPM for top-of-the-page banner ads, which meant that 100,000 pageviews per week were no longer enough to earn a profit from a site that employed professional journalists and editors. Many news sites gave up and closed. Others hung on, hoping for a turnaround of some sort. But hardly anyone in the business was making money. Too many had based their business plans on 1997 or 1998 ad rates, and their expenses had gotten so high that there was no way they could ever make money without ads rates going back up to where they were in "the good old days."

Those days are not going to come back. From now on, Web sites planning to earn the bulk of their living from advertising must face the fact that they will have to live with rates comparable to those charged by their offline competition for similar exposure.

Perhaps, as seems to be the case with book publishing, the future of ad-supported Web publishing belongs to the very large and the very small. A small group of journalists whose material is unique and interesting enough to appeal to at least 100,000 daily readers, and who have either plenty of sales ability or enough sense to team up with a competent marketing person from the very start, may be able to earn a living putting out online news, and large, well-financed publishers can probably make a go of the business if they are extremely canny about every step of their Web activity and are very cost-conscious, but the in-between arena may never be profitable, especially for purveyors of general, as opposed to niche or industry-specific, news.

Tech News as a "Natural" for the Web

The type of online news most likely to make money today and in the foreseeable future is news about computer hardware and software. This is obvious; by definition, anyone who reads news online owns a computer or computer-like device which he or she uses to connect to the Internet. That computer or device is going to wear out sooner or later, even if "wear out" means only that the case gets grungy or the monitor gets a bit dim rather than a catastrophic failure. Where better to advertise computers than on computer screens? And what kind of news site could be more likely to attract computer industry advertisers than one carrying news about computers and software?

This does not mean you can put up an ill-conceived site that lists or reviews Windows programs and suddenly have advertisers beating down your virtual door and waving million-dollar banner ad contracts in your face. All it means is that a tech-news site has a better chance of survival than one that can't define its audience closely.

But you must also realize that there are plenty of tech news sites out there already, because the "Computer information is a natural for the World Wide Web" thought is neither new nor original. Almost every major computer-oriented trade magazine publisher moved online to some degree or another between 1994 and 2000, and almost every one of them pulled back heavily between the summer of 2000 and the end of 2001, because after online ad rates plummeted these publishers could no longer afford the large staffs they had accumulated during the easy-money years. Hundreds of sites closed in 2000 and 2001, and layoffs among tech journalists were so massive that the whole industry suffered as hard as a steel town whose biggest plant has shut down.

Do you really have a unique idea for a site? Is it one that is likely to attract enough users to make it worth selling advertising on—at $2 or $3 per thousand banner ads you display? Can you keep your costs low enough to pay all your expenses and make a profit too? What if the company that hosts your site suddenly raises its rates 15%? Will you still be okay? What if, out of three writers you hire, one turns out to be a "star" whose work generates two-thirds of your traffic—and another publisher suddenly offers her 30% more than you are paying? Will you be able to match that offer? Playing "What if?" in a negative direction is a gloomy game, but any person in any business who doesn't play it regularly is liable to be wiped out by even a minor negative change in business conditions.

Tech news publishers, online or offline, must be prepared for downturns as well as good times, just like any other business. Sadly, an awful lot of people who go into tech publishing, especially on the Web, are optimists at heart. Give them a chance of a prayer of a profit, and they're off and running, hiring everyone in sight who can string a coherent paragraph together and knows the difference between Windows and Linux. If you are serious about doing tech news online, and plan to build a site or group of sites that will last more than a few years, you are probably best off putting together a small group of aggressive reporters and editors and running a small number of accurate, leading-edge stories instead of trying to flood your site with material regardless of quality. When the advertising market is healthy, it's easy to think you need to maximize the number of new pages you publish in order to maximize revenue, but that same expansionist thinking is what gets you into trouble whenever the ad market tanks, as it does every time there is a hint of an economic downturn.

The tech news market—from the advertising side, which is what really counts—is a highly volatile one. It is also one in which it is easy to latch onto a new technology that seems to be rising fast, figuring that you are going to catch hold of a whole bunch of new revenue, only to find that you were not the only one who had this bright idea.

Linux reporting is a prime example of this problem. Linux, a community-created computer operating system, was all the rage from about 1997 to 2000, literally the fastest-growing operating system in the world. The only thing that grew faster than the number of Linux users was the number of Linux-related publications. Almost every possible domain name shorter than 25 characters that had "Linux" in it got registered, along with most of the ones that contained the words "tux" or "penguin" ("Tux the Penguin" is the Linux mascot) or anything else even remotely related to Linux or its open source relatives, the BSD Unixes. For a while it seemed like the first thing every new Linux user did after he or she got Linux working was put up a "Linux News" page of some sort. In most cases, once the thrill had worn off, those sites stopped being maintained and just sat there, sucking up search engine referrals that otherwise could have gone to useful sites into which continuing effort was being poured. Now the wave of new Linux "news" sites has abated. Linux continues to spread (and is still the world's fastest-growing operating system), but it is no longer a fad, and there are established sites which most Linux and open source software users know about and rely on for the bulk of their Linux information, so there is little room for new ones to draw more than a few hundred daily pageviews unless they offer something radically different from what is already out there.

What applies to Linux news applies to all other niche or specialty tech news publishing, on or off the Internet. Publishing entrepreneurs and established publishers start new ventures to cover the new technology, and before long two-thirds of these efforts die, leaving a small corps of stalwarts to thrive—or at least survive in a marginal fashion —with their futures tied to that particular technology's ups and downs.

You Are Not C|Net

When C|Net bought ZDNet, it became the most prolific online tech news and info purveyor ever. You want Windows software downloads, they've got them. Mac games reviews? Got those, too. Linux discussions? For sure. Inkjet printer price comparisons? Of course. Duplicating the breadth of their coverage would cost millions of dollars, and chances are you would never make that investment back, let alone see any return on it.

The Genesis of NewsForge

As Linux and Open Source (and Slashdot's) popularity grew, Slashdot got an increasing number of reader requests to cover more Linux and Open Source news and do less coverage of "frivolous" things like movies, toys, and wing-ding science. Instead of yielding to this clamor, which came from a small percentage of Slashdot readers, and turning the site into something it was never meant to be, in early 2000 we decided to make an entire new Web site that would be the "online newspaper of record" for Linux and Open Source.

The initial concept was a simple site that would do nothing but display headlines and brief summaries of stories published elsewhere about our chosen topic areas. Jamie McCarthy, a programmer who also wrote articles for us part-time on Slashdot and was writing real-time search software in his day job, joined us full-time to write a program called NewsVac that would scan hundreds of other news sites, all over the world, looking for key words like "Linux," "BSD," "Open Source," and others that seemed appropriate. Our intention was to log every single Linux-related story published online, anywhere from Linux Weekly News to the Singapore Straits Times, that was relevant to our target readers.

Then came a little ethical question: If we viewed online news publishing as a huge "pot" of stories, what right did we have to dip into that pot without putting something back in? There is no legal problem doing this; we weren't republishing work published elsewhere, just linking to it, and links are the essence of the World Wide Web. But it still didn't feel right. So I cast about a bit, and hired Grant Gross, who had ten years of newspaper reporting and editing experience, plus two years of online writing behind him, as NewsForge Managing Editor. Tina Gasperson, who was already writing for us on several sites, joined Grant on NewsForge. We had several freelance columnists who had been working on a previous, non-Open Source news site, along with several part-time editors to cover our NewsVac feed and write brief link-story summaries on nights and weekends when Grant and Tina weren't around to do it.

But Grant's main job was to produce real, newspaper-style coverage of as many events pertaining to Open Source, Free Software, and GNU/Linux as possible. There was a need for this kind of service. Most online Linux news coverage at the time was fanzine-like, with little hard-core reporting going on. "Gosh, isn't Linux great? We love Linux s-o-o-o-o much!" was nice to say now and then, but a constant diet of it was not useful to readers who needed a clear and accurate picture of what was going on in the Linux and Open Source communities, especially from a business perspective.

I figured it would take at least a year to get our coverage up to speed; initiating coverage in a new, specialty business area takes time and work, hard-core contact-building, and a body of institutional knowledge, plus it takes time to build reader credibility for any publication that is trying to provide insider coverage of a comparatively small, "everybody knows everybody" community. And even after its rapid post-1997 expansion, the Linux community was still tiny compared to the Windows-using crowd.

But Grant and Tina amazed me by starting to routinely produce credible Linux and Open Source breaking news coverage less than six months after NewsForge was launched in August, 2000, and by the time the site celebrated its first anniversary it was averaging about 30,000 pageviews on weekdays, plus another 40,000+ readers for the two daily newsletters we generated from its constantly changing content.

In early 2002, we took the radical step of putting our underperforming _Linux.com_ site under direct control of the same editorial team that had done so well with NewsForge. It proved to be an excellent decision. Three months after we relaunched _Linux.com_ with a new look and new personnel, the combined reader-ship of _Linux.com_ and NewsForge was averaging at least 150,000 pageviews per day and climbing steadily.

NewsForge Financial Projections

My original financial projections for NewsForge were based on an average ad banner sale price of $5 per thousand pageviews, with five banners per page and 80% of ad inventory sold, or $20 in gross income per 1000 pageviews. This was considered exceedingly con-servative when I drew up the orig-inal NewsForge plan in early 2000; our (then) publishing VP was confident that he could get at least $20 per 1000 pageviews per banner and sell all five on each page, for a gross income of $100 per 1000 pageviews. Based on my projection of 25,000 pageviews per weekday and 10,000 on week-end days by the end of NewsForge's first year in exis-tence, this would have given the site $754,000 in gross annual income vs. a budgeted annual operating cost, once it was up and running, of (roughly) $350,000. These are the kind of numbers we all like to see!

My original combined budget for NewsForge's development and first year operating cost was $500,000, and I dolorously assumed no income at all during this period. Without a minimum budget commitment of $500,000 I was unwilling to build the site, despite all the optimistic sales department input I was getting.

I sadly got to say, "I told you so," during much of 2001, because NewsForge ad banners—like ad banners on other sites—did not sell as rapidly (or for as much) as pre-recession industry wisdom (wisdumb?) had predicted. I had set my budget based on the possibility of a sharp decline in online advertising activity. I didn't predict a recession; I just allowed for one, figuring that if we really were experiencing an endless boom (which I really didn't believe was possible), the site would make a ton of money, and if the economy tanked, we'd be able to survive without backing away from my original vision of NewsForge as the world's most complete source of Linux and Open Source news.

Projections are nothing but guesses, of course, and mine were neither better nor worse than anyone else's. NewsForge site readership grew more rapidly than I expected. Advertising sales were less robust than I expected, but the ad

rates which we were able to get did not drop as precipitously as they did for many other online publishers, in large part because the type of news coverage which NewsForge provided proved attractive to a demographically ultra-desirable IT upper management audience segment which no other site reached as directly as we did. And now, as I write this in mid-2002, premium "top of the page" ads on NewsForge are selling quite well, and we are working to achieve that same state of grace with *Linux.com*.

Reader Feedback as a Secret Weapon

All the financial projections really did was give us a "go/no go" decision point and a budget base. They told us that, in order for the site to survive no matter what happened in the advertising marketplace, we had to keep our editorial staff small and server and bandwidth expenses to a minimum, which we did. We did not have good numerical data, at the beginning, about exactly what content we should provide. What we *did* have was several years of experience running Slashdot, *Linux.com*, freshmeat, and other Web sites popular with Open Source developers and users. This was (and is) a vocal crowd, and we have always listened to what its members say with totally open ears. I personally received (and still receive) anywhere from

500 to 1000 reader emails per week, and I *read them all*.

This high level of feedback acceptance is the secret of NewsForge's success. Indeed, it is the secret of all OSDN sites, and why it seems like we know exactly what our readers want and who they are even though we rarely do formal readership surveys.

What we learned from NewsForge readers, almost immediately, was that they liked our original reporting more than the NewsVac feed. Sure, they appreciated our links to virtually every on-topic story, announcement, or press release published anywhere on the entire World Wide Web, but they considered our in-house reporting, hardware reviews, and weekly columns the site's most attractive features. Our response, naturally, has been to gradually increase the number of original stories we publish.

We have also learned that we wander beyond our original Open Source/Free Software reporting niche at our peril. Every time we have published anything even a little bit outside this self-imposed mandate, we have gotten an earful from readers. In effect, we have an editorial board with thousands of members who keep us on the straight and narrow. While we don't take every suggestion we get seriously, when we hear the same complaint—or compliment—over and over again, we sure as bleep

pay attention. We also take the source of a comment into account; if it comes to our *editors@newsforge.com* email address from the CIO or CTO of a large company that uses Linux heavily, we are more likely to listen to it than if it comes from a high school student who is thinking about installing Linux for the first time. But a reader's potential purchasing power is not everything. If an email suggestion about Slashdot content comes from an accounting manager at an international consulting firm who knows little about technical matters, we are less likely to take that reader's advice than we are to take advice from a 25-year-old programmer doing freelance projects for local small businesses, because that programmer is part of Slashdot's core target audience and the accounting manager is not.

Listening carefully to our readers—and just as carefully choosing which readers to listen to—gives each of our sites a distinct identity, direction, and readership. But listening is not something you do for a little while, then stop doing once you feel you've gotten enough feedback, because both readers' and advertisers' needs change over time. Could we decide, at some point, that it is better to combine NewsForge with *Linux.com* than to maintain it as a separate site? We might—if enough of our readers tell us that's what they want.

So, if C|Net is so all-encompassing, why bother to put up a tech news site at all? Answer: because even though malls have department stores that sell "everything," there are plenty of other retailers in the mall that make a decent profit by offering items the department store doesn't carry. The same thought can be applied to tech news Web sites.

Do you love digital cameras? Film cameras? Both? Have strong opinions about them? Have enough background as a photographer or technician to back your opinions with facts? Then you might have a fighting chance to make a few bucks with a site concentrating on photography—not that there aren't plenty of digital and film camera news and information sites out there already—if you can come up with a unique take on the industry, one with a more personal flavor than C|Net's.

There are hundreds of little niches in tech news, each of which has potential for someone who is willing to work hard and has something interesting to say. A site dedicated to one of these little niches isn't going to attract millions of readers, but one run by one or two people just might be able to make money. And if those people figure out how to run one specialty site at a profit, even if that profit is tiny, they can then start another one using their accumulated expertise and the infrastructure they put together to make the first one, and do it again...and again. Some of these sites will fail to attract an audience and will need to be cut loose. Others may do well. It's a "throw enough mud at the wall and some of it is bound to stick" situation. (It's also possible that none of the mud will stick, but that's a risk you take in any business.)

Beyond Tech News: General Media Online

The precepts are the same for mainstream news online as for tech news: You need to find an information niche which no one else is filling well, and develop a targeted audience that at least some advertisers will pay a premium to reach.

An obvious niche is geographical; newspapers and local broadcasters are natural online news outlets, but many seem confounded by the World Wideness of the Web and have trouble using it effectively as a local medium. This is changing as journalism schools and industry organizations like the American Press

Institute pay more attention to online news delivery—and how to profit from it.

Another obvious way to target a news niche is by topic or special interest. *FreeRepublic.com*, a grassroots conservative political news and discussion Web site, has attracted an ardent enough (and large enough) following that reader donations cover its entire operating budget.

A third popular method of targeting a news Web site is to pick out a constituency like women or college students. But targeting groups whose members may not have much in common beyond sex or age is a tough job, and advertisers have not shown much inclination to pay premium rates to sites with such loosely defined readership demographics.

So far, the most successful method of targeting online readership seems to be by topic. Rap music listeners, automotive performance buffs, and frequent moviegoers all represent definable non-technical interest groups attractive to specific advertisers. Note that picking out an audience defined by its probable interest in purchasing a specific group of products or services is the most profit-centric way to build a Web site. It is a concept that follows naturally from the idea, discussed in Chapter 1, that from a business perspective a news Web site is an ad delivery vehicle that uses editorial content as a way to get readers to look at ads, not a vehicle for content that "just happens" to have ads on some or all of its pages.

Moving Offline News Online

There are several major headspace changes needed for broadcasters or print publishers trying to expand onto the Internet. The two most important changes follow:

1. Each member of your online audience controls the order in which he or she views your site. It is better to think of a Web site as an information index built on the principle of information layering than as an online version of what you are already doing in print or on the air.

2. A local publication or broadcaster competes only with other local publishers or broadcasters. This is not true on the Internet, where readers are only one click away from NBC,

The New York Times, *Financial Times*, and every other online information source in the whole world. You had better have something unique to bring to the online table or no one is going to be interested in your Web site when he or she can just as easily get the news from a world class source as from yours.

Okay, so you're producing a local TV news show. Assuming you're a network affiliate, you might as well get your Web site's national and international content from your network. The cost of duplicating their coverage would be insane. But what you can do on your site, that your network—and CNN and *The New York Times*—can't do, is provide background for local stories you report, essentially information layering, with your over-the air story being the first layer. Try this:

1. Run a 30-second on-air story about a zoning controversy on the west side of downtown, with a standup report from the City Council chamber. Subtitle: "more at" *ournewssite.com* and a voice announcement, "Learn more about today's zoning dispute at *ournewssite.com*" at the close of the story segment.

2. Place a headline and summary paragraph on the front page of *ournewssite.com* that approximates—or is—the on-air story script, with a "read more" link attached to it.

3. On a separate page on your Web site, supply deeper background information. This information should include links to City Council transcripts and public zoning records if they're available.

4. The online version of the story should contain a photo or two (video capture is okay) of City Council members and other parties involved in the zoning dispute. Put thumbnails (very small photos) on the main page of the site in order to keep loading time reasonable, and larger versions on the page for that particular story. If budget permits, make a streaming video clip or two available—in RealPlayer format, because RealPlayer is the only online streaming media software that is available for almost every popular operating system in use today.

What we've done is use the on-air story as the first information layer, with that layer essentially duplicated in text on the station

Web site's front page. Readers who aren't terribly interested in this story can glance past those few brief words and go on to other stories, while those who want to know more about zoning can click on a link and get either a deeper, more complete story (the one you'd have aired if you had more time available for it) and links to public records that go into great and tedious detail. Plus—assuming you have the budget to produce and deliver streaming video—you offer video clips that both include and go beyond the on-air story.

Following this pattern gives your viewers a number of choices, depending on their level of interest in this story. You have provided not just news, but a fully-layered information resource about a story that *The New York Times* is unlikely to cover (unless you're in New York, of course), and you have created unique Web content that gives your audience a reason to use your Web site.

Follow this same procedure over and over, day after day, and your site will develop a following that will make it worth your ad sales force's time to market your Web site to local advertisers, either on its own or along with on air sponsorships.

A newspaper site can do the same thing, perhaps replacing a TV station's streaming video clips with links to stories the paper has previously published about the subject of today's story. Some newspapers charge to retrieve older content and some don't, but it is probably good practice to make links to older stories that are directly relevant to today's story free for site viewers who get to them by following links from your most recent headliners.

Besides linking to your own material, link freely to relevant material published elsewhere. Some Web publishers worry about sending site visitors away. Don't fall into this trap. If your content is viable and even-handed, your site users will come back. Comprehensive lists of links to outside sources, especially public records, academic studies, and other in-depth information produced by non-journalistic entities, will accentuate your publication's reputation for honest and all-encompassing news delivery.

The Standalone News Site

So, after all this depressing talk, you are going to open a news site not connected to any other medium—or try to keep one you already own alive. Look at some of the characteristics shared by some of the more successful ones:

- Drudge Report: Tiny staff, large readership.
- *News.com*: Large staff, huge readership.
- TheRegister: Small staff, large readership.
- Wired News: Small staff, large readership.

You get the pattern. Large staff and a small readership simply won't cut it. Most of the sites noted above focus on tech news, but they could as easily focus on other areas traditionally neglected or barely covered by general-audience media. The Drudge Report is an exception; it covers... well, whatever it is it covers, but the Webmaster does it with hardly any help at all, and his all-text site uses next to no bandwidth or server space so his technical costs per reader are negligible. Drudge can sell ads for a dollar or two per thousand and make money.

You could do worse than following one part of Drudge's original "recipe," and starting out as a one-person operation. It might be even better to have two people: one to do the reporting, and one to do the marketing, with the marketing person focusing primarily on building an audience until you start getting around one million pageviews per month, and on advertising sales after that. Keep graphics to a minimum, search out a reliable, low-cost Web site hosting service, and your salary, plus your partner's if you have one, will be your only sizable outlay. If you have enough savings or outside capital to live for two years, plus $1,000 or so per month to pay server bills and other expenses until you get some ad money coming in, that's all you need to get your site going. Whether you start turning a profit before you run out of capital is subject to many uncontrollable factors, but if you follow the site design precepts laid out in this book, and you are a diligent reporter providing unique coverage of an area that interests enough people to provide you (and prospective advertisers) with enough eyeballs to make ads on your site valuable, you will have a fighting chance.

Ultra-Niche, High-Value News

A strategy for creating a profitable ad-supported news site that isn't used often, but has been used successfully by several small online publishers and is gradually becoming more popular, is to concentrate on a tiny news niche, one that may attract only a few thousand or even a few hundred readers whose attention is extremely valuable to a similarly limited set of advertisers.

This Web site business model assumes that you have specialized knowledge of a particular industry and are willing and able to cover that industry in more depth than anyone else. An example might be a site that reports on government building regulations that affect the construction of high-rise office towers—not when those regulations are enacted, but when they are first proposed. This site would be promoted, on the reader side, only to decision makers in national and global construction firms. For specialty construction equipment manufacturers, this is a golden audience; cost per thousand readers is not a valid way to set ad rates for it. A maker of (for example) specialized tower cranes that sell for $500,000 or more may be willing to pay thousands of dollars per month to sponsor your site even if your average daily readership is measured only in the hundreds. Accumulate five sponsors, each willing to pay $5,000 per month for a link from your main page to their sites, and as long as you keep your staff small and your quality high, you will have no trouble earning a decent living.

This is not something just anyone can do. To pull it off you must have name recognition in your field among both readers and prospective sponsors. If that field is international-scale construction, a test might be whether the president of Caterpillar will take your calls. If so—and if you can get him and a few other major construction equipment vendors to sponsor your site—you will be able to make this work.

What if you're not a noted expert in a field like construction law or another one that might lend itself to a "premium audience" site, but are a skilled, Web-hip promoter and entrepreneur? Fine. Accumulate a stable of experts in different fields and make a series of premium sites. You do the sales and marketing, and provide hosting and business services, while your experts provide the editorial content. Your experts aren't going to work for free or purely on percentage. No one who has a strong reputation in a high-stakes field needs to take that kind of risk, so you must take the need to pay substantial authors' fees into account when you set up your business plan. At least, by running multiple sites, you will spread your risk. Allowing a one-year "make or break" cycle for each site is probably prudent. If you have not been able to locate appropriate sponsors for an "expert site" after a year of trying, that site might as well be written off. But if you set your margins correctly and keep your expenses under control, you don't need every site you create to become profitable. Ideally, you should allow for a site failure rate as high as 80% when you first set up this business. This is a pessimistic view, but if you allow for the worst and get the best, it is better than the other way around.

Subscription News Sites

The Wall Street Journal's *WSJ.com* claimed 591,000 subscribers on June 30, 2001, but like almost everyone else in the online news business, *WSJ.com* laid off staff that year.

Salon.com started selling subscriptions in April, 2001, and, according to some sources, had 12,000 subscribers by the end of June. At $30 per year per annual subscription, that's $360,000. But at the same time Salon was boasting about its subscription program, one of its founders was quoted as saying the company was "running on fumes," and that the only reason it was going to survive was that it had picked up $2.5 million in new investment capital. Salon was still losing money at a horrific rate—like $2.9 million per quarter—despite the subscription revenues, and in several public interviews Salon executives said total revenues were down 45% from 2000.

At the same time, *FuckedCompany.com* "one-man band" owner/editor/publisher Phil Kaplan claimed he was making $1 million per year, mostly from $75/month subscriptions, working from home with only one assistant. Phil said his trick was that he was posting only about 10% of all the (negative) business news and rumors submitted to him on the public section of his site, and gave access to all of his content only to paid subscribers. Before he started selling subscriptions, Phil relied on nothing but advertising revenue for his income. And, he said at the time, he hardly made enough money to eat from ad revenue.

SearchEngineWatch.com, founded by Danny Sullivan in early 1996 as "A Webmaster's Guide to Search Engines," and part of *Internet.com* since late 1997, has a free area that carries user-level information, but charges for access to a private section of the site that gives professional Webmasters and site promoters deep insight into the listing methods and operations habits of search engines. Sullivan has said, in several casual email exchanges over the years, that *SearchEngineWatch.com* is consistently profitable, even though the same has not always been true of _Internet.com_ as a whole.

There are enough other subscription sites out there that listing them all would take more pages then there are in this whole book. The common factor shared by the ones that make money is that they all offer specialized information and insights that are not available elsewhere. Most are run or figureheaded by one or two strong personalities, and subcriptions are promoted aggressively on the free sections of their sites, and by making sure the site's figureheads either write plenty of articles for other media or are quoted heavily as "industry experts." Another common tactic is to have a site's "stars" give plenty of presentations at industry gatherings in order to enhance their "expert" status yet further.

A notable example of a site that follows this pattern is _www.useit.com_, where Web design and usability guru Jakob Neilsen holds forth. The site's major free feature is Neilsen's popular biweekly _Alertbox_ column. There is also a list of recent interviews Neilsen has given. And then we come to the meat of the site: a list of highly-specific usability reports you can _pay to download_ for prices that range from under $30 into the hundreds. Neilsen says repeatedly that ads on Web sites do not work, and says this is why his site doesn't carry any. Yet when you come right down to it, _his entire site_ is an ad for his publications and the services of his consulting firm, the Neilsen Norman Group. Make of this dichotomy what you will, but Neilsen certainly makes money, not only from selling reports online, but from lecture fees, consulting work, and book sales. He has staked out a business niche where he has special expertise, and has marketed himself successfully within that niche. It is a niche filled with people and companies that can and do directly use Neilsen's advice to help increase their bottom lines, so he can charge substantial sums to share his considerable knowledge without potential customers balking at his prices.

Neilsen doesn't sell subscriptions per se, but sells articles one at a time. In fact, he is dubious about fixed-rate subscriptions for Web sites in general, except for a few "must read" trade publications that have nearly captive audiences. He cites _Variety.com_, the online edition of the famous entertainment industry daily, as an example of a site for which a paid subscription model makes sense.

Salon.com is another well-known Web site that has been moving toward a subscription-based revenue stream. Even so, it may never make money. It is filling an online niche (literary journalism with a strong liberal bias) that has never been much of a profit provider for print magazine publishers either. Perhaps Salon, like many magazines that serve the same market offline, would be better off if it looked for direct financial support from wealthy individuals or foundations that believe in what Salon is trying to do and want to invest in its future for non-pecuniary reasons.

Perhaps _WSJ.com_ should have little or no staff of its own, and would be better off if Dow Jones looked at the Internet primarily as an alternate delivery medium for the "print" _Wall Street Journal_ instead of trying to produce a significant amount of online-only copy for _WSJ.com_, and marketed the online _Wall Street Journal_ primarily to people who live in areas where the print version is hard to get, and to readers anywhere who prefer reading downloaded material on their computer screens to cluttering their desks with paper, instead of treating it as a separate publication at all.

Another possibility more Web publishers may want to consider is delivering subscriber-only material in email newsletter format. Industry- and topic-specific subscription newsletters delivered by postal mail have thrived for decades. Moving this concept to the Internet does not take a major mental stretch. Indeed, many successful postal mail newsletter publishers have already moved either partly or completely online.

Chapter 6, "Email and Chat as Profit Builders," will talk about email newsletters in more detail.

Email and Chat As Profit Builders

Most talk about business use of the Internet centers around the World Wide Web, but email and, to a much lesser extent, chat and instant messaging, are also effective profit-building tools. In some cases they can be far more valuable than a Web site, although they tend to work best when tied to a Web site instead of trying to stand on their own.

Responding to Customers' Email

The simplest and most basic use of email is to answer inquiries from customers. Email has the advantage over telephones in that it does not occur in real time; if you take one minute to answer a phone call it is a long time, but if you take an hour or even a day to answer email, customers will generally accept the delay. Customers who live or work more than a few time zones away will often find email more practical to use than phone calls because they can send you email at any time instead of trying to find an hour when both you and they are at work. This time-shifting ability, combined with a written record at both ends, was a big reason teletypes were often used, instead of telephones, for intercontinental business communications back in pre-Internet days.

Think of email as a nearly free teletype service that doesn't require a big machine that makes loud chunk-chunka noises all day long and you'll have a handle on its most basic use.

Email can also replace faxes. The transmission cost is lower, and because it doesn't take a separate phone line to send or receive email, no one should ever get a busy signal when trying to send an email to you, which is a distinct possibility when you rely on a fax machine as your primary (written) electronic communications device.

You should figure on 24 hours or one business day as the longest acceptable time to respond to sales or general customer service email. Acceptable tech support email time limits depend on the nature of your business. Obviously, if you are selling a product or service which people depend on to run their business, an hour can seem like eternity to your customer.

Reporters on deadline also need rapid email responses. Fail to answer email from the media almost immediately and you risk seeing the dreaded "[your name here] could not be reached to respond to the allegations" line in print or on a respected industry news Web site. Reporters may not be customers, but in effect they represent customers and prospective customers, often thousands or hundreds of thousands of them.

Email is a cruel master in a way postal mail has never been, but it is less demanding than the telephone, and less expensive than fax service. It also offers temptations which other means of communications do not.

Resisting the Lure of Spam

The message in your email inbox offers to send your advertising message to millions of qualified or "opt in" email addresses for a few hundred dollars. Compared to the cost of outbound telemarketing or direct mail, this is an insanely low price. The temptation to use "the power of email marketing" can be almost overwhelming to a promotion-minded businessperson on a tight budget. But resist this temptation you must, because the proliferation of Unsolicited Commercial Email (UCE), colloquially known as "spam," has become an ugly, cancerous growth on the face of the Internet.

It is easy to tell yourself that you are not a spammer just because you send a couple of emails to a few million strangers—that your message, unlike all the email junk you get, is of vital importance to at least some of the people who will receive it. But you are wrong. You are still sending spam. Indeed, most people who have used the Internet for any length of time have learned that the phrase, "this is not spam," in the body of an email means that it almost certainly is spam, just as a sign at a nightclub's door that says, "no motorcycle club colors allowed," tells you the place is a biker hangout.

Perhaps if unsolicited commercial email had been used more widely by major companies making legitimate offers when the Internet first went commercial, it would be accepted (or at least tolerated) and not be derisively known as spam today, but this did not happen. Just as the U.S. "900" telephone billing arrangement was originally intended to let legitimate information providers charge for their services as part of users' phone bills but was co-opted by porn services almost immediately and tainted forevermore by that association, the first major users of bulk email promotion were pornographers, multi-level-marketing hustlers, "chain letter" swindlers, hoaxers, and other dubious characters. If you send spam, you are forever associating yourself with these people in potential customers' minds.

Using Opt-In Promotional Email

Let's start by talking about the difference between opt-in and opt-out. Opt-out email is what you send people who didn't check a box that said "I don't want to get email from you." In other words, you are assuming the right to spam them unless they specifically tell you not to. All the MLM, porn, and penis enlargement spammers make this same assumption. If you are on their ethical level, go ahead and use opt-out email marketing, the kind that says, "You are receiving this email because…" and offers a method of unsubscribing either directly by email or by clicking onto a Web site that offers an unsubscribe utility of some sort. Perhaps you feel that this "opt-out is bad" attitude is wrong, and that it is good business to send promotional email to people who bought a product or service from you or took some other action that put their email address into your hands, and didn't bother to specifically tell you not to send them promotional email. Perhaps, in a world where nasties weren't using email to promote garbage, you would be right, but we live in a world where they have poisoned opt-out email so badly that no legitimate business can use it without at least some customers or potential customers getting offended by all unsolicited email.

The only legitimate, totally accepted mass marketing use of email currently available is the "opt-in" list, and the people to whom you can send this kind of email without negative repercussions are those who have knowingly opted in to *your own company's* offerings either by sending email to you asking to be placed on your email list or by entering their email address in a form on your Web site and clicking a "subscribe" button. Even the "subscribe" button method is not foolproof; a common online problem is pranksters who subscribe people they don't like to hundreds of email lists, which forces the victims of this kind of prank to spend hours or days unsubscribing, and tends to make those victims angry at the companies from whom they get all that email. The way you protect your reputation from this sort of shenanigan is to require all subscribers to respond positively to a "Did you really mean to subscribe to our list?" confirmation email you send to them. Adding the confirmation email to the subscription process makes it, in industry parlance, "double opt-in." Once someone has replied positively to the confirmation email, you can be reasonably certain that they really want to hear from you, at the frequency and in the manner specified in your original sign-up information.

Another major courtesy for your email subscribers is to give them a choice between plain text email, which they are likely to prefer if they are on slow dialup connections or in countries where Internet access is charged by the minute, and HTML email with pictures, which they may prefer if they have unlimited, broadband Net access (Figure 6–1 shows a signup page with many choices).

Yet another courtesy is to make it easy for subscribers to alter or even cancel their subscriptions. The best way to do this is to put a line like this at the bottom of each email you send to a subscriber:

Click Here to change or cancel your subscription.

Honesty with subscribers is also important. If they sign up to receive a weekly software review, that's what you must give them. You can't suddenly decide to send them a daily list of "red-hot

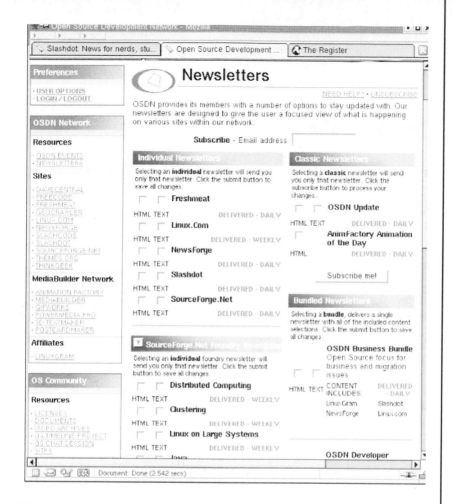

Figure 6–1   Many choices available, including choice of delivery format. This makes readers happy.

inkjet cartridge specials," and say, "Well, you opted in to receive email from us," as a justification for this obnoxious intrusion. Selling your email lists is another edgy area. It looks like a good source of short-term income on the surface, but customers tend to dislike it immensely.

Once customers find you have violated their trust by abusing their email addresses in any way, they are unlikely to trust anything you tell them, and if they don't trust you they probably won't buy from you. Worse, if the people whose trust you abuse are involved in any online email or chat groups, they may spread tales of your perceived perfidy far and wide. You are far better off, in the long run, having a small but loyal group of email subscribers than having a huge list of people who get email from you and your business associates that they don't really want.

News As Email

Any newspaper, television station, news Web site or other news outlet can and should have an email newsletter option, and ideally more than one. A newspaper, for example, can put out a newsletter aimed at sports fans that is topped by the latest sports stories and scores, with other news headlines below. The same newspaper can also put out a local news update, a national news newsletter, and several others, possibly including a TV "daily highlights" piece, simply by rearranging existing content. This costs nearly nothing to do once the basic template has been set up; dozens of Open Source and commercial programs are available that will automatically generate email newsletters based on human-set rules. This intense targeting is good not only for readers who have a specific set of interests, but gives ad salespeople a set of special, high-value sponsorship opportunities which they can offer to both new and existing clients.

Readers will not sign up for newsletters they do not know about, and advertisers will not sponsor them without a concerted, long-term sales effort. Successful newsletters do not happen overnight or without major investment of time and other resources, any more than newspaper or magazine subscribers magically appear out of thin air. Any news outlet that wants to see newsletters become a strong part of their business needs to promote them constantly, just like any other subscription-based service. Even a free email newsletter demands time from readers, and that time may be more precious to many of them than a minor subscription fee.

Just as a Web site that is promoted in print must promote associated print, or broadcast products in return, an email newsletter should help push readers or viewers toward your Web, print or broadcast offerings. Email newsletters can directly promote ad inserts in newspapers, for example, with Friday's email mentioning inserts scheduled to go in Saturday's paper. A local retail advertiser for whom an insert is a major investment might be willing to pay an extra fee to have that insert promoted via email. Or, if necessary, an offer to promote an insert or other major campaign with a special round of free email newsletter advertising might make a great deal-closer when an ad salesperson is dealing with a recalcitrant client—and may create additional single-copy paper sales, too.

Email newsletter distribution may be instant—you either click "send" or your system automatically sends newsletters at a predetermined time and they're in subscribers' email inboxes a few seconds later—but you can never forget that the humans who decide to subscribe are no faster than the humans who subscribe to newspapers and magazines or watch TV. You will not build an email subscriber base overnight. It can take a year, possibly two or three, to get enough subscribers to make an email newsletter profitable.

How many subscribers it takes to earn that profit can vary so much from newsletter to newsletter that there is no way to come up with an easy formula for it. Obviously, a newsletter that runs nothing but stories culled from an existing Web site is going to cost much less to operate than one that runs original material. Ad rates can vary wildly depending on audience demographics and the skill levels of the people selling those ads. All these factors must be taken into account. Subscription build rates, too, can vary wildly depending on the intended audience and content, and on marketing cleverness and persistence, as can the number of people who unsubscribe for one reason or another and must constantly be replaced just to keep your subscriber numbers stable, let alone make them increase.

Emailing news can produce excellent profits, either directly through paid advertising placed in the newsletters themselves or by using emailed news to build Web site readership or, ideally, both. The big trick is to set up newsletters for the long haul and grow them gradually, rather than trying for a "big bang" start and being disappointed when they don't start pulling in major money right away.

Maintaining Credibility in Email Newsletters

At one newsletter extreme, you have subscription-supported publishers like G2 computer intelligence news. Their money comes purely from their readers. They have no reason to give those readers anything but complete and unbiased news coverage.

G2 Computer Intelligence Earns a Good Living from Paid Subscribers, Not Advertising

Charles Hall is president of G2 Computer Intelligence, a publisher of paid subscription email newsletters. G2 has been in this business since 1989 and has been consistently profitable. G2's current single-reader subscription rate is $595 per year, per newsletter, although many subscriptions are sold to groups or even entire companies at much lower per-reader rates.

In March, 2002, while many online publishers were worrying about whether they would survive, G2 launched a new title, *Epostal News*, covering ecommerce and how it affects national postal authorities, along with coverage of the companies that supply ecommerce software and services to post offices. Within four weeks, the U.S. Postmaster General and other top officials of the United States Postal Service had subscribed, along with executives at other countries' post offices and, said Hall, a surprising

number of people from what he calls "the competition," meaning private carriers like UPS, Federal Express, and DHL.

EPostal was a spinoff from G2's already-established *The Online Reporter*, a newsletter that covers ecommerce industry news. Hall said G2 was getting enough interest in—and enough stories about—ecommerce matters directly related to postal authorities that they felt there was market room for a newsletter that covered nothing else. This move also took post office-specific news out of *Online Reporter*, and allowed that newsletter to focus purely on ecommerce in private industry.

"Focus" is one of Hall's favorite words. Ask him how to duplicate G2's success, and he'll tell you, "Stay focused. Work hard."

The first G2 publication, in 1989, was called *UniGram*. It covered the then hot/new shift in the computer server marketplace from vendor-specific mainframe operating systems to Unix. When Microsoft introduced Windows NT, and it started looking ■ like a potentially viable competitor to Unix, G2 launched *Client Server NEWS* to focus on Microsoft's attempt to enter the systems and networking market.

The Online Reporter was started in 1996 because G2 saw the need for a hard-core "insider scoop" newsletter covering ecommerce. And now *EPostal* (see Figure 6–2) has spun off from *Online Reporter*. Hall does not discuss potential future titles, but several are always under consideration.

about the complex topics that they cover. Seasoned industry professionals like Maureen

Figure 6–2   The PDF version of *EPostal*. G2 newsletters are available in text, HTML, and PDF format.

Reporting Is Hard Work

Hall says the reason G2 succeeds in selling newsletter subscriptions while other news outlets covering the same market niches have trouble building readership on Web sites that do not charge for their content is that G2 does original, hard core, investigative reporting; that instead of rewriting press releases, G2 reporters are constantly on the phone and exchanging email with direct contacts within companies they write about. "It all boils down to hard work," he says. "And we don't let rookies write reports

O'Gara, founder and executive editor of G2, work the phones and trade shows and stay in constant contact with industry decision-makers."

Asked if others could duplicate G2's journalism success, Hall says, "Sure, if they want to work as hard as we do."

Selling Subscriptions Is Hard Work, Too

G2 sells subscriptions as aggressively as it reports. Walk into the company's Glen Cove, New York, office at almost any hour during the business day, and you will see at least one or two people busily calling potential subscribers, asking if they would like to receive a free trial subscription to one of G2's newsletters. After the potential subscriber has received free newsletters for three weeks, he or she gets another call. This time he or she is asked to convert to a paid subscription.

G2 does not buy contact lists from other publications. It searches business directories for names, and goes to trade shows to collect contact information in person from exhibitors and attendees. The G2 Web site (*www.g2news.com*) also offers trial subscriptions, but not through an online form. You must email or call. This puts you in direct contact with a G2 subscription representative, and also puts that subscription rep in touch with you so that you can be called and reminded to convert your three-week trial subscription into a paid subscription when the trial ends.

This is a well-developed, simple, but very clever sales pattern. Not every prospect buys, but enough do that G2 earns steady profits even in tough economic times.

Hall says others could do exactly what G2 does on the sales side, just as they are free to duplicate G2's reporting efforts. But he points out that it takes constant effort to make G2's sales system work, and that G2's success has not come overnight, but has taken years to build.

At the other extreme, there are email newsletters that are nothing but promotions for a single company, that are all about that company's products or services and are obviously intended to either directly sell those products or services or to keep exiting customers loyal. There is nothing wrong with this kind of newsletter. Readers know what they are getting.

The problem comes when a company sends out what is essentially a promotional newsletter, and includes an edited industry-specific or general headline news section or tries to hide the fact that the newsletter is a promotion instead of unbiased news. No sane corporate manager is going to publish a newsletter that runs a review saying a competitor's product is better.

Perhaps it's possible to run news of interest to customers and potential customers that doesn't mention either your company or its competitors, but doing this makes no sense. The whole point of publishing a newsletter for customers is to talk about your products or services; to tell them about special deals or upcoming promotions; to give them product and service updates and usage tips; to make them feel that they are loved and that you care about them, and that you see each one of them as more than a one-shot source of money.

A corporate-published newsletter for customers should have only one purpose: building a continuing relationship with those customers. It is exactly the same as a corporate Web site in this regard, although newsletter subscribers are more likely to be loyal customers than Web site visitors, because anyone can click onto a Web site for a second, but your email subscribers went out of their way to make a connection with you. Make your newsletter an excellent source of information about your products or services, and you will be giving them exactly what they signed up for—and making them into even more loyal customers in the process.

Email Discussion Lists

An email discussion list can be a great tool for communicating with employees, a useful but risky tool for communicating with distributors or franchisees, and a downright dangerous way to establish a dialog with customers.

When employees post to a corporate-owned email list using their company email addresses, you know who is posting. There is an unspoken assumption that management has access to the list, and it is best if that assumption is not unspoken, but management is obviously there, communicating with the entire company, possibly issuing regular "from the top" announcements, encouraging discussion of the latest pronouncement, and actively participating in those discussions. This is the modern, white-collar equivalent of the plant manager or company president wandering around the factory floor, talking casually with the workers. It is also an astoundingly inexpensive and effective way to unite employees who work at different locations into a single, coherent team.

Most Net-hip companies already have many email lists, each for a different purpose. Software developers on a particular project can and should have their own list to deal with that project. Salespeople for a particular product line should have their own list where they can exchange sales and product tips—and even a bit of general gossip, especially if many of them are far from the main office and work alone and the email list is their primary contact with their peers and managers. Plant managers and maintenance people who work in different cities or countries, but use some of the same equipment, may need and want an email list where they discuss the machinery under their care. The only kind of corporate email list you rarely see is one called "general chatter," and perhaps more companies should have one like this, dedicated to no particular topic, that is nothing but gossip, birthday announcements, personal notes, and even pictures of children and grandchildren. Naturally, you don't want anyone spending excessive time in this sort of non-productive activity, but a little bit of it can enhance cohesiveness and help people remember that they do not work in a vacuum or only as part of a small group, but are part of a large operation full of people who all have their own dreams, motivations, tasks, and personal lives. Bonding is good. Without it, there is no company with a coherent mission, just a lot of isolated individuals or small units, all working without knowing or caring that they are part of a whole.

Monitoring casual email chatter can tell management a great deal about employee morale and can even, if the monitoring is done adroitly, help spot problems that might otherwise go unnoticed. If some of your email lists start getting lots of requests for help from co-workers with a specific piece of software, for example, you have just spotted a need for better training or, perhaps, a bad piece of software that needs to be reworked or replaced with something less cumbersome. But in the meantime, at least people are helping each other learn how to use the software. If it's a new program that everyone is learning, not something hopelessly flawed, the email list becomes a casual, user-to-user support channel that takes a lot of heat off your Information Services staff.

An email list for independent distributors or franchisees is, on the surface, much like one for employees, except that you have less control over what they say. If an employee posts inappropriate material to a company email list, you can discipline that employee, but if a distributor or franchisee feels he or she has a gripe which you do not feel is valid, and posts it to an email list where other distributors or franchisees can see it and perhaps take the complainer's side in the dispute, how will you respond? Just as rumors can spread wildly and uncontrollably on the Internet at large, an open email list populated by people who are supposed to be your business partners and allies can suddenly turn into a rumor mill, or worse, into a virtual mob attacking the parent company.

Okay, you can run a *moderated* email list, where each post is approved by a company representative before list subscribers can see it. Then you reject a complainer's post. "You are censoring me!" he or she says, followed almost inevitably by the statement, "I have a right to say what I want!"

Yes, you are censoring that user. You really have no defense against that charge. The post you didn't allow to go through may have charged that your company's software product caused harm to wild dogs in Australia or something equally silly, and that may be the reason you censored it, but you are now cast in the role of Bad Person, and suddenly there is a new complaint against you. What do you do now? Allow the posts complaining about censorship to go to all list members? Do that, and you create questions about the original message you refused to post. There is no way you can win this argument short of closing down the entire email list, and if you do that, and the complainer—possibly with help from a friend or two—digs up the email addresses of his or her fellow distributors or franchisees, you may find yourself faced with a renegade email list that does nothing but criticize you and your company. The net result is stress and anguish. You will wish you had never created an email list for your distributors in the first place.

You probably shouldn't have created an open forum for distributors or franchisees. The safest course is to put out a regular email newsletter for them instead of running an email list. This way, you have complete control over what is published, and that control looks (and is) absolutely legitimate. You can publish selected emailed complaints and questions in the newsletter, along with your responses to them, and answer others privately.

You can't keep disgruntled distributors or franchisees (or disgruntled employees, for that matter) from setting up their own email lists or online forums, but there is no reason you should help them do it.

Every danger associated with open email lists for distributors or franchisees is multiplied for customer email lists. If you have 100,000 customers and a 99% customer satisfaction rate, that means you have 1000 dissatisfied customers. If you set up an open email list for customers and publicize it effectively, at least a few of the upset 1000 will post to it, and it takes only a few people with vitriol in their bellies and time on their hands to make an unmoderated email list useless for everyone else. A moderated list is safer, and a newsletter that publishes only selected customer comments and questions is safer yet.

The only exception to all of this is an email list associated with a news Web site or newsletter that has no vested interest in any particular product or company. A news-oriented email list can do little or no harm to the publisher that sponsors it, and may be simpler and less expensive to set up and operate than comment-posting facilities on a Web site, especially for niche publications that do not have and may not even want large readership numbers.

Thoughts on Email List Management

Newsletter subscriptions lists can be any size, but there may be practical limits to email discussion lists. The classic rule of thumb is that about one out of six online bulletin board or email list denizens posts regularly, while the rest "lurk," which means they observe instead of participating. An email list with 60 subscribers can therefore be expected to have 10 members who post actively, and "actively" can range anywhere from once per week to several times per day depending on the list's topic and the amount of passion the members have for it. How argumentative they are can also be a factor, but let's assume they are generally civil people who don't get into long back-and-forth exchanges where they all call each other names a dozen times every day, but stay on topic and speak up only when they have something useful to say. But one daily post from each of 10 people is still 10 daily messages. To some Internet users, that is a negligible amount of email. To others it's a lot. In any case, it's a manageable number.

Now multiply list membership by 10, to 600. If the 6:1 lurker:poster ratio holds, and each active poster averages one message per day, suddenly your email list is up to 100 daily messages.

How many Internet users have the time or stamina to deal with that much email on a single topic? At 30 seconds per message, that's 50 minutes per day—nearly an hour—spent reading email generated by that email list alone, and an active Internet user is likely to receive plenty of other important email, plus his or her share of the growing amount of spam that flows through the world's email servers like cancer cells through a leukemia victim's arteries.

When an email list starts taking up too much of subscribers' time, some of those subscribers will leave. The problem is, the subscribers who leave may not be the ones doing most of the posting, and the ones who stay may not be the ones doing the highest quality postings. An unmoderated email list can self-destruct if this happens unless a "list manager" monitors it regularly, participates, and gently guides discussions. This brings up a time and/or money problem, because managing an active email list can easily take several hours every day.

Is this amount of work worth your while? It can be, if the list supports a specific piece of software or another product, and the list takes at least some load off of technical support personnel, but in that case you must deal with the potential problem of a few unhappy customers turning the list into nothing but a complaint venue, and ruining its original purpose. The only sure way to prevent this (and keep the list on topic and the number of messages on it manageable) is to restrict list membership to registered users of the product or another defined group, and to make sure each member reads and agrees to a set of rules before joining. Anyone who violates the rules and won't fall back in line after several gentle reminders from the list manager must be banned. Some may try to come back again under a different name or through a different email account. This is why limiting membership to registered product users or using some other identifier besides an email address to keep just anyone from subscribing can be a good idea.

Even some news media should consider restricted or "invitation only" email lists. Imagine, for example, a hypothetical publisher who specializes in news for the hydroelectric power industry. The readers whom this publisher serves are government and utility executives, large-scale construction contractors (dam builders), and heavy equipment manufacturers. This is a geographically dispersed industry, so an email list would be a great way for people in it to get to know one another and share their problems and concerns. The publisher would be doing his or her readers a great service by providing and managing such a list, and would probably find it a great source of story leads as well. But this list will not work unless it is strictly private, because if it isn't, members won't feel free to speak their minds. The hydroelectric industry is often controversial; it is often the recipient of large amount of government funding, and it is often embroiled in disputes with environmentalists and competing power producers. A hydroelectric power generation executive may not want to speak openly on an email list that may be monitored by coal company people or environmental activists—or reporters. But even a closed email list should not be considered truly private, especially if messages posted to it are archived on a Web site, as seems to be the case with the vast majority of email lists.

Email Is Never Private

An email list dedicated to technical support should be archived, and the archives should be available on a Web site, and easily searchable, so subscribers can look at old questions and answers instead of wasting other list members' time asking about something that might have been covered a few days or weeks ago. An email list where ideas are exchanged among a group of professionals probably should not be archived. But the lack of archives does not mean that email messages sent to a group are truly private, since most companies log and save all email that runs through their corporate servers, and courts, at least in the U.S., can subpoena those messages, and members of an email list can certainly store messages on their own computers. In the end, privacy on an email list, and even in private email, is an illusion unless that email is encrypted and the encryption keys are tightly held by a small group of people who are all sworn to death if they are captured by "the opposition," whoever that may be.

The terms of service for any email list or group you start or run should make the inherent lack of privacy in all email very clear to subscribers.

But most of all, you need to remember, yourself, that your own email is not very private, whether you send it to an email list with 5000 members or to a single co-worker.

Chat and Instant Messaging As Business Tools

On the customer service front, imagine a tool that requires excellent typing skills while demanding the same response speed as telephone service, and you have online chat. What's the point? To save on long distance bills? That's the only reason that using chat instead of the telephone can possibly make sense, but with bulk long distance costs now well under three dollars per hour in the U.S. and many other countries, your hourly labor costs had better be awfully low if chat-based customer support is going to produce measurable savings over phone support.

It seems, on the surface, as if capitalizing on the growing popularity of online instant messaging or chat services as a customer contact mechanism makes sense. Perhaps it does, if your objective is to look cool to people—especially teenagers—who love instant messaging. But in a practical sense, you are probably far better off using a combination of telephone and email responses for sales support and customer service.

Consider:

- Instant messaging demands an instant response. A customer who clicks on a "Chat with a company representative now" link expects to chat with a company representative *right now*. Leave that customer waiting for more than a minute or two and it is not "instant" messaging or "live" chat. Are you willing to devote enough staff to live chat response to assure message lags of no more than a minute or two at *all times*?

- A telephone customer service rep must have a clear, easily understood speaking voice. A "live chat" customer service rep must be able to type not only rapidly, but accurately. You will need to screen email reps for spelling and writing ability, and to maintain the "instant" promise implied by "instant messaging." You do not need people who can construct intelligent essays if they are given hours or days to write them, but people who can turn out near-perfect material as quickly as an old-time newspaper reporter working against deadline. Are you sure you can recruit and retain enough people with these skills to make live chat viable? Are you willing to pay enough to attract people who have these skills—in addition to the other skills (including endless patience) which a customer service rep must have?

- Most telephone customer service reps read all or part of their responses from scripts shown on a monitor screen. In theory, a live chat operator can paste appropriate sections of those responses into the chat input and send them directly to the customer instead of reading them out loud, and this saves time. But does it? What about your customers? Are they all speed readers? Many people cannot read as fast as they can listen, and in typed chat it is harder for them to ask for clarification of a word or phrase than if they are talking to your rep by phone. This introduces yet more delays.

- Chat is not only dependent on your reps' ability to write clearly, but on customers' ability to form questions clearly and type them coherently enough that your reps can understand them. Again, requests for clarification take time.

"Chat live with a rep right now" is one of those things that looks good on the surface but is hard to implement. Its greatest utility is probably not in customer service, but as a method of generating sales leads. Instead of picking up the phone (or in the case of people who have only one phone line which they use for both voice and computer, *logging off* before calling), a customer can express interest immediately and, hopefully, get a near-immediate response. Probably the best response is along the lines of, "I'm Brian, your sales rep. Why don't you call me so we can discuss this further? My direct phone number is. . . ."

Instant messaging is not nearly as suitable as email for sending step-by-step instructions to a customer, and since it is usually easier to paste a prewritten message into an email message blank than an instant messenger form, email is a much more practical medium for technical support. Plus, as stated earlier in this chapter, there is the time factor; customers do not expect you to reply to email nearly as rapidly as they expect you to respond to instant messenger or "live chat" queries, which makes email a lot easier to handle.

Besides, if a customer has a problem which he or she needs to be solved right away, isn't a reassuring *human* voice on the other end of a phone line a lot nicer than anonymous text in a little box on a computer screen?

Viruses and Other Email Hazards

The most obvious day-to-day email hazard is time-wasting. Spam is a growing irritation that wastes bandwidth on corporate networks, and angers people on dialup modems who have to wait for the junk to download so they can get their real email, but spam rarely wrecks anything. Viruses, on the other hand, can do serious damage either to an individual computer or an entire network. There

Internet Chat as an Internal Communication Tool

As I write this, I am logged into four different IRC (Internet Relay Chat) channels, all for work. One is used by _Linux.com_ and _NewsForge.com_ editors to discuss story ideas and edits, one is for technical matters pertaining to those sites, one is for _Slashdot.org_ editors and programmers to use for both editorial and programming discussions, and one is for loose social chat. It is called "slashdot-cooler" because that IRC channel is our online equivalent of a casual "water cooler" conversation.

Of course, the people who work on _Linux.com_, _NewsForge.com_, and _Slashdot.org_ are not all in the same office. Today I've seen users log in from seven U.S. states, Canada, Australia, England, Israel, and Germany. Some of them are full-time staff employees, and some are freelancers. Some are writers, some are programmers, some are sysadmins. IRC (see Figure 6–3) is our meeting ground, the glue that holds our distributed work force together.

We prefer IRC, which is generally considered pretty geeky, because we're geeky people who run Web sites for geeks—and because it's free. We have set up private channels (password required to join) on an existing, volunteer-run IRC network with which we have some casual connections. We talked about setting up our own in-house IRC server at one point, but decided it was easier to use existing, outside infrastructure instead. We have only about 30 people who work directly on our Web sites (writers, editors, programmers, sysadmins) and communicate rapidly and constantly with each other, and even a minimal IRC server running Linux can handle several thousand users.

Companies or work groups that aren't full of technical people may prefer other instant messaging services to IRC; there are certainly plenty of them around. ICQ (_www.icq.com_), AOL Instant Messenger (_www.aim.com_) and Yahoo! Chat (_chat.yahoo.com_) tend to have the best cross-platform capabilities among the well-known ad-supported commercial services; that is, you can use them in Linux, Mac, and

Windows, while others may cater only to users of one or two major operating systems and leave some of your people out of the conversation.

under your control rather than being subject to the whims of another company. There is also Open Source Jabber (_www.jabber.org_) available at no cost for those who have the technical skills (and time) to run their own servers, and would rather do it themselves than hire an outside company to handle it.

It's probably best to ease gradually into live chat or instant messaging as an internal communications method instead of issuing an edict one day that says, "This is how we are going to talk to each other from now on." OSDN never formally decided to use IRC chat. It was, and still is, a grassroots thing, first adopted by one small group of workers, then by others who saw how well it worked for the first group and decided to jump onto IRC themselves.

The one big problem with live chat is that it can be addictive. _Highly_ addictive. In our corporate case, where we all work online for

```
x | + | < | > | LCR 4/17 1 AM T_2_3_0_21 % http://www.salon.com/comics/lay/2002/04/16/lay/
pudge    hehe                                                          o  6 | c  0 | 20
pudge    at least CNN included a "?"                                   o CaptTofu
jamie    http://slashdot.org/~Rupert/journal/3282                      o CowboyNeal
jamie    pudge: I have these Debian packages installed that seem to    o jamie
relate to what you questioned about:                                   o KmdrTaco
jamie    libfreetype6-dev, libfreetype6, freetype2                     o krow
jamie    libjpeg62-dev, and libjpeg62 (strangely marked for removal    o pudge
but never gets removed)                                                axehind
pudge    ok                                                            CmdrBoto
pudge    i'll install libfreetype                                      Gamara
jamie    ha. "apt-get --simulate dist-upgrade" says I have 185         hemos
updated packages and 10 new ones coming to me                          jamie_
pudge    downloading from SF.net is way slow                           jellicle
--> KmdrTaco (malda@cloaked.tnt3.det5.da.uu.net) has joined            kdeqc
#slashdot-authors                                                      neth
-- ChanServ gives channel operator status to KmdrTaco                  roblimo
pudge    ok jamie, CD is insalled                                      robo
jamie    woo!                                                          samzenpus_
pudge    passed all tests but for XPM which we don't need, surely      sproul
pudge    ok, now i guess i install the plugin                          tim_tn
pudge    hum                                                           toad
--> hemos (~hemos@12-232-255-109.client.attbi.com) has joined
#slashdot-authors
pudge    where is it?
pudge    slashdot CVS?
jamie    will be shortly
jamie    found a bug... fixing
pudge    install-plugin for it, right?
pudge    (once i get it installed)
pudge    can this go in slash CVS, or should it be private?
--> axehind (brian@vpn-route.osdn.com) has joined #slashdot-authors
jamie    it's going into the main CVS, yes
jamie    ok, lemme know when
jamie    hey did you commit that messages verbosity change? I'm
still seeing the mesasge delivery errors in slashd.log on Slashdot      Op    | DeOp
pudge    did you restart slashd?
jamie    yeah, of course                                               Ban   | Kick
jamie    we're at verbosity 2...
pudge    just checking.                                                Sendfile | Dialog

roblimo
```

Figure 6–3 Programmers use IRC to discuss changes to the software that runs _Slashdot.org_.

Large public chat or instant messaging services, including IRC networks, are too insecure to use for exchanging critical information. A company called Jabber (_www.jabber.com_) sells private corporate chat and instant messaging services that are far more secure than the public ones, and an additional advantage of going the Jabber route is that your instant messaging will be totally long hours anyway, this is not a problem; we keep our chat programs going in corners of our screens, and need only to take a fast scan of the channels we're on every hour or so, because most of us have set our chat programs to beep at us whenever we get an individually-addressed message. For workers who aren't online all day as part of their jobs, or those who aren't "chatted out" most of the time because chat is an all-day, every-day work thing for them, the temptations of social chat can be big barriers to productivity, even if that socializing is only within the company. Social email can be a time-waster, but live chat's instant feedback (assuming the person on the other end responds instantly most of the time) can lead to conversations that occupy hours even though the people holding them might feel like they've spent only a few minutes typing or reading in those little chat program boxes in the corners of their computer monitors.

are thousands of viruses "in the wild," with new ones constantly getting written.

Almost all email-borne or Internet-spread viruses—technically most of them are "worms" but we'll use the vernacular here—affect only computers running Windows, and the Microsoft Outlook and Outlook Express email programs are famously susceptible to them, so the simplest and most obvious way to protect against viruses is to connect to the Internet only with computers that run Linux, Mac, or Unix, not with computers running Windows. Linux, especially, is nearly virus-proof because its Open Source code makes viruses easy to spot and stop, if not for everyday users, at least for the millions of programmers who prefer this operating system and keep a close eye out for any problems with it—and usually distribute cures for potential security flaws which they find in Linux before those flaws can be exploited by the nasty people who write viruses. The underlying code for Mac OS X is also Open Source, so it, too, is unlikely to be as virus-victimized as purely proprietary operating systems.

Those who prefer proprietary "closed source" operating systems must constantly be on guard against email viruses. They must use virus scanning software, and that software must be kept up-to-date, not just bought and ignored after the purchase, because there are always new viruses.

Several other safeguards:

- Never open email attachments from anyone you don't know, and be suspicious of attachments from people you do know unless the body of the email describes each attachment precisely, by name and content. The reason you must be watchful of even your best friends, assuming they use Windows, is because a bad habit of many highly effective email viruses is to email themselves to everyone in an infected computer's email address book, and you are more likely to be in friends' address books than in strangers'.

- If you or your company own your own email server, even if it runs Linux or Unix and therefore cannot get infected with Windows viruses itself, you should still have virus detection and rejection software installed, because if any of your co-workers are running Windows on their desktop computers, and those computers get infected and start emailing large files automatically, the additional traffic volume can slow your network to a crawl or even make it stop from the overload.

- Outlook Express, Outlook, and Microsoft Internet Explorer users must disable ActiveX, because it is the "key" many viruses use to gain control of their computers. There are control panel settings in each of these programs where they can do this.

These three precautions will take care of most email virus problems. The same "never open unknown attachments" rule also applies to instant messaging services that allow file transfers. These, too, can be virus carriers.

Email and Chat Are Changing, Not Static

Telegraphs, telephones, teletypes, and fax machines all changed the way business was done. All of these technologies have had both good and bad aspects, and all took time to absorb. Fax is still new enough that questions about whether it is proper to send unsolicited faxes are still in the U.S. courts, and what we might call "fax etiquette" is nowhere near as well-developed or universal as the basic style and format of a business letter sent by postal mail.

Email does not yet have any standardized etiquette or set of widely-accepted salutation and signature styles for business or personal use, besides the universally-recognized belief that using excessive capitalization is the online equivalent of shouting AND IS CONSIDERED THE HEIGHT OF RUDENESS BY MOST EMAIL USERS!!!

Chat is still free-form, based on "Hey dude! Whazzup?" informal one-line or two-line conversational snippets, often with many words and phrases (such as IMHO, "in my humble opinion," or BTW, "by the way") abbreviated.

Postal mail started in the days when only a small percentage of the population could read or write and was used for centuries with absolute formality, with most recipients addressed by their titles even in the most casual communications. Email's roots are in the informal world of t-shirt-wearing programmers who called each other by first names even if they had PhDs, and they often didn't bother with a salutation at all since the automated "sent by" and "recipient" headers in email contained all the information they needed to identify each other. Instant messaging and live chat have been driven by an even more informal culture: teenagers talking to other teenagers. In teenage chat, complete sentences are often rare, and "gr8" can mean "great," so that many chat conversations take place in code almost impossible for outsiders (like parents and other adults) to understand.

For businesses dealing with customers, a bit more formality is probably in order. Some businesses that sell heavily to teenagers and want to seem like they're up with (or down with) the latest trends are trying to use "hip" email and chat argot in their newsletters and on their Web sites, but this tactic ends up making them look as silly as a middle-aged man with a potbelly wearing clothes better-suited for 19-year-olds. You, hopefully, are smart enough to avoid doing this sort of thing—unless you are 19, communicating one-on-one with a customer via live chat, and you sprinkle your chat interchanges with teen-style symbols as a matter of course both at work and at home. And even in this case, you may want to come across as just a bit more dignified than the average teenager, so you're probably better off sticking to standard spelling and grammar.

It is easy to think that just because email and chat are cheap and easy to use, you don't need to put any thought into the messages you use them to send. This is not true. To a customer, that email you dashed off in a few seconds is you and your company. Spelling counts. A courteous mode of address is always in order, even if it's just a simple "Dear Dan," and nothing more than that, on friend-to-friend emails, and "Dear Mr. Daniels" when corresponding with a stranger. A signature is important, even if it's just a little "Bill" separated from the email's main body by a single blank line—and, naturally, you should sign email to strangers with your full name and title, not just your first name; the first-name-only signature must be reserved strictly for email to people who already know who you are.

Email subject headers are also important. We need to start paying more attention to them, in order to make them more accurately reflect the contents of our actual messages than we did in the past. Part of this necessity has been pushed upon us by spammers who use "Hey!" and other folksy, seemingly familiar subject lines to make us think we're getting a message from a friend instead of an unwanted pitch for life insurance or a porn Web site.

In the absence of defined email and chat styles, your best bet is to do the same as you should do with technology: Stay behind the leading-edge curve instead of trying to keep up with it. Let others be pioneers and try new things while you plod happily behind them, imitating their successes and trying to avoid their failures.

The Most Important Email and Chat Rule

Many businesses seem to treat email or other online communications from their customers as something they are forced to accept instead of realizing that they are possibly the greatest ways ever developed of getting customer feedback. The ease of sending email or typing out a brief chat message may mean you end up getting a lot of nonsensical questions that people wouldn't bother you with if they had to send you a postal letter or pick up a phone to ask, but keeping a close eye on customer email or chat can give you useful input which you might not get any other way. Even "stupid" questions may be telling you that your Web site or other material needs to be revised so that customers understand it better, or even that your products need to be redesigned so that they are easier to use.

An email address like "*suggestions@yourcompany.com*" can give you the online equivalent of a high-priced marketing study without any direct expense at all.

Monitoring outside email lists related to your business can give you even more feedback.

Investor relations people now routinely read through online discussions about their companies' stocks. You can and should also monitor online product and service discussions, especially email lists that relate to your business in some way. These lists, and associated Web site and online bulletin board discussions, can serve not only as the most unbiased feedback sources you could ever hope to find, but also as a source of information about your competitors.

It takes time and patience to gather and interpret mounds of email, chat, and other incoming online information. If you don't have time to do it yourself, hire someone who does. If your business is generating enough online feedback and discussion that it takes more than a few minutes a day to process all of it, that feedback is important enough to be worth paying someone to read, absorb, and summarize for you. For a large company, several salaries spent monitoring online discussions can save millions in potential losses by catching and allowing management to respond to just one false product or financial rumor before it spreads beyond a small email group into the mainstream media. The same is true for smaller businesses, although on a smaller scale, and instead of salaries spent it may be the owner's time.

Web sites and newsletters are how you talk to customers. Email is how customers talk to you. If you fail to listen, you are throwing away half the advantage of using the Internet in your business.

If there is any one rule for using the Internet as a business tool that you should paste up on your office wall, let it be this one:

"The Internet is a dialogue, not a monologue."

Site Promotion and Advertising

Not all of the hundreds of millions of Internet users in the world are going to be interested in your Web site or newsletter, so get those big numbers out of your head and focus strictly on the people who are valuable to you as site visitors or newsletter subscribers. Concentrate all your promotion efforts on them, and them alone.

Depending on your business, you may have a target audience of anywhere from a few hundred up into the millions. Your job is to reach that audience, not the rest of the Internet. The most obvious and basic way to do this is to make sure your site is correctly listed in appropriate Internet search engines and directories.

Directories Are Not Search Engines

A search engine searches the World Wide Web for Web sites and pages and extracts information from them. It files links to all the sites it scans in a single, huge database, based on key words it sees on those sites. Readers then use search words or phrases to tell the search engine what sites in the database they want to view.

A directory cuts its database into sections. Instead of finding sites by search word match, users are given category selections, then subcategory selections, and possibly sub-sub-category selections.

There are major differences between these two creatures. A search engine is the best tool to use when you know what you want to find. If you know you are looking for "Bill's Garage in Peoria," a search engine that does a good job of keeping its listings up to date will come up with Bill's Web page, if he has one, or a directory listing of some sort that will give you Bill's phone number and address. But if you have a broken Volkswagen and want to get it fixed but have no particular garage in mind, you might be better off browsing than searching, and directories offer better browsability than search engines. For example, you might go to a directory that is organized by geography and find its "Peoria" section, then look for an "automotive repair" subsection. Once you're at that point, you can select which garages you want to check out—including Bill's, if his is listed in that particular directory.

The biggest problem with online directories is that all of them are incomplete. The best ones are compiled by humans, and that makes them expensive to maintain. Directories tend to be more reliant than search engines on submissions to keep their databases current, and this opens another window where human uncertainty can creep in, especially when it comes to culling outdated links. Hardly anyone ever bothers to email all the directories where his or her site is listed to say, "We're going broke and taking our Web site down, so please remove all our listings, thank you."

Simple Tricks That Help Get Favorable Search Engine Rankings

There are plenty of services that claim they can get your site displayed among the "top 10" in search engine listings for chosen key words. This is always true only if you choose an obscure word like "xantipodeanismatic" or something equally unusual or made-up. Choose a word like "sex" and you'll find that you aren't the first one to think it would be a good word to use in bringing traffic to your site. The funny thing is, unless your online business activities are directly sex-related, "sex" would be a poor keyword for you, even if

The Biggest Search Engines and Directories

These are the most popular general-purpose search engines and directories, according to most Web rating firms' figures. Rankings change, but this bunch, listed here in alphabetical order, almost always holds the top spots.

AllTheWeb
http://www.alltheweb.com

AllTheWeb has one of the most complete indexes of all Web pages. In theory, AllTheWeb will eventually list your site whether you submit it or not, but it has a submission page, so you might as well. It takes only about 10 seconds and costs nothing.

AltaVista
http://www.altavista.com

AltaVista has been around since 1995 and shows its age in some ways, but it's still popular. As of February, 2002, you were allowed to submit up to five URLs for free and hope they would get listed within four to six weeks or pay varying amounts, starting around $40, for faster service and listing enhancements of various types.

AOL Search
http://search.aol.com/

If you're an AOL member, you get a version of AOL Search that includes AOL's internal content. The rest of us get only access to non-AOL Web content. There is no point in submitting a URL to AOL Search. It uses listings from Open Directory (below) and Inktomi (also below). Submit to them and if your listings are accepted, they'll automatically show up on AOL Search.

Ask Jeeves
http://www.askjeeves.com

Submitting to Ask Jeeves is tedious and bound by many rules. The Jeeves trick is that readers are supposed to ask questions in natural English, like "Where do I buy a new CD player online?" and are supposed to get answers, like "From *buyCDplayers.com*." This means that instead of simply submitting a URL to Jeeves, you write answers to potential reader questions. Jeeves also has "partner sites" whose listings appear among the regular listings, in addition to sponsored links shown above the regular listings. Jeeves also shows search results from other search engines, including Overture, which charges for listings. Ask Jeeves gets less traffic than MSN, AOL, Lycos, Google, Yahoo! or Go.com, so you may not want to pay much attention to it.

Direct Hit
http://www.directhit.com

This one barely makes the list of big search engines, but submitting to it is fast and free, and Direct Hit results may also appear on other search engines, so it's worth your time.

Google
http://www.google.com

Google should be your number one submission priority. It is a popular site not only because it has one of the most complete indexes of the Web's content but also because it consistently gives readers accurate search results. The key to getting a high rank in Google is having as many other sites as possible link to yours. Since Google continually crawls the Web for new and updated pages, in theory yours will eventually get indexed even if you don't directly submit it, but a submission may speed up the listing process. Sites listed in Google also appear in Yahoo! and Netscape searches. The Google submission page is not easy to

find from the site's main page, so here's the URL: http://www.google.com/addurl.html.

HotBot
http://www.hotbot.com

Submitting to HotBot is fast and free, and HotBot submissions often find their way into the Inktomi database, which is a nice feature because Inktomi charges to accept direct submissions. HotBot search results come from Direct Hit, Inktomi, and the Open Directory project, so submissions to them will also get your site listed on HotBot.

iWon
http://www.iwon.com

iWon is a "portal" that happens to offer a search feature. It gets traffic by offering readers a chance to win prizes. The more times they click on iWon, up to set limits, the greater their chances of winning. If your site is listed by Inktomi or you have signed up for Overture's "pay for performance" service, your site will automatically appear in iWon searches.

Inktomi
http://www.inktomi.com

Inktomi sells search services to others and doesn't have a search page of its own. If you're willing to pay $39 per year for one URL and $25 per additional URL (as of February 2002), Inktomi will crawl your site or sites every 48 hours so your listings will always be up to date. Inktomi provides search results to AOL, iWon, MSN, HotBot, and NBCi, among others.

LookSmart
http://www.looksmart.com

Don't even think about getting listed in LookSmart's human-edited directory unless you have $149 or more to spend (as of February 2002). If you are willing to pay for search engine listings, there are better ways to spend your money.

Lycos
http://www.lycos.com

Lycos grabs listings from AllTheWeb and the Open Directory Project, but also accepts free submissions at *http://home.lycos.com/addasite.html.* It shares ownership with HotBot, but the two sites operate independently.

MSN Search
http://search.msn.com

MSN Search gets its directory listings from (pricey) LookSmart and its search results from Inktomi. Since MSN search is currently the default search in Microsoft's Web browser, it is worth some attention. You can submit a commercial site free at *http://submitit.bcentral.com/msnsubmit.htm* for inclusion in the general search

results, which are shown below the paid listings.

Netscape Search
http://search.netscape.com

Netscape's directory takes all its listings from the Open Directory project, which Netscape owns, and its search results come from Google. List in these two, and you're in Netscape Search without any other work.

Open Directory
http://dmoz.org/

This is a human-categorized directory that relies on volunteer editors who each agree to maintain listings in at least one category. There is high editor turnover, and some editors work harder than others, so the time from a site's submission to its inclusion in the directory can vary widely, depending on the section of the directory to which it is submitted. You can, of course, always volunteer to become an Open Directory section or category editor yourself—and make sure your own listing is always correct and up to date.

Overture (formerly GoTo.com)
http://overture.com/

This is a "pay for performance" service. You and other submitters "bid" for attention by offering to pay a set amount per referral to your sites. The one willing to pay the highest amount goes at the top of the list shown as the result of a keyword-based search or directory section, and the one with the lowest bid is at the bottom. After all the paid listings, you see free listings from Inktomi. The top bids in some categories are over one dollar per click. In others, there are no paid listings at all.

Yahoo!
http://www.yahoo.com

Once the undisputed king of Web directories, Yahoo! hasn't been maintaining its listings as well as it should. Apparently manage-ment has been concentrating on other site features, like free email, chat, clubs, and so on. Yahoo! is still one of the world's most popu-lar Web sites and is the most pop-ular independent portal (the other two top-ranked portal sites are MSN's and AOL's home pages, which are the first ones all their users see when they log on), but it seems that less of Yahoo!'s traf-fic goes to its directory or search than it did a few years ago. Yahoo!'s search function is Google's, repackaged, so a Google listing will get you at least some Yahoo! visibility, anyway.

it brought lots of traffic to your site. If you sell lawn mowers, you're more interested in being found by people searching for "lawn mowers" or "garden supplies" than those looking for anything else.

The most obvious place for a search engine to pick up keywords from your site is in your text. Since many search engines read only 100 or 200 words into each page they scan, having words people are likely to use as search terms right up top on each page is impor-tant. For a garden center, it might be a good idea to have the first words on your site be, "Ralph's discount lawn and garden supply— lawn mowers and parts—seeds and fertilizer—all kinds of lawn and garden tools and equipment—discount prices—serving Bradenton, Florida, residents for over 25 years."

This statement doesn't need to be large. It can be rather small type, and below it you can have a typical logo or a major headline of some sort. But what we just did, by adding a line of carefully chosen "top" copy, is make your page a little more search engine-friendly than one that starts with random words.

Let's think for a moment like a person using a search engine to find a new lawn mower.

The obvious phrase he or she ought to type in is "lawn mower," either as two words connected with a Boolean "AND" between them to make sure they get pages that have both words in them, or with the pair of words enclosed in quotation marks so that they get pages that contain those two words next to each other. But most Internet users are not sophisticated searchers; few probably even know how to use Boolean expressions (which are special algebraic terms used heavily in the binary arithmetic that governs the way computers work). That's okay; search engines allow for people who don't have deep computer knowledge, and if someone types "lawn" and "equipment" as separate words, it is likely that a page that has the words "lawn equipment" close together at or near the top will be displayed ahead of one that contains the sentence, "We were out on the lawn, wrestling with sound equipment for Dori's party."

If your hypothetical searcher (your prospective customer) is in Bradenton, Florida, and uses either or both of those two words as part of his or her search, you now come out on top of all the garden supply stores and lawn mower dealers in the rest of the world. You have the word "discount" in there in case someone thinks to put that one in, and you are also primed to get attention from people looking for "fertilizer" or "seeds" or even "garden tools."

There is no way you can anticipate every word that someone might use to find a business like yours on the World Wide Web, but you can easily cover the most common ones in a sentence or two. Not only that, since one way that search engines rank sites is by how often key words appear on them, and if you sell lawn mowers and garden supplies you are going to have words related to those products throughout your site, the added words up at the top increase the chance that your site will be one of the first ones your prospective customer sees.

Now let's increase your chance of getting attention by using your site's <title>, <description>, and <keywords> effectively. They're in brackets here (and on your site) because these words are meant only for machines to read, and enclosing them in brackets keeps them from being displayed by your prospect's browser. You can get quite detailed with these "metatags," as they are called. Here are the tags from the DaveCentral software archive site:

```
<title>[DaveCentral] - welcome to DaveCentral,
   Software Archive</title>
<meta http-equiv="Content-Type"
   content="text/html; charset=iso-8859-1">
<meta name="description" content="DaveCentral
   Software Archive is an
```

```
extensive listing of Internet shareware, free-
    ware, betas and demos for
Windows 3.X and Win95, all free downloads.">
<meta name="keywords" content="shareware, soft-
    ware, freeware, anti-virus,
browser, browsers, compression, editor ,editors,
    email, ftp, news readers,
irc, telnet, screen savers, anti virus, windows,
    utilities, download,
plugin, plug-in, plugins, winsock, 32-bit, 32bit,
    graphics, multimedia,
telnet, vrml, authoring, Shareware, Software,
    Freeware, Anti-virus,
Browser, Browsers, Compression, Editor , Editors,
    Email, FTP, News Readers,
IRC, Telnet, Screen Savers, Anti Virus, Windows,
    Utilities, Download...
```

. . . and we'll stop here, because there are hundreds more, mostly minor variations on spelling and capitalization so that
DaveCentral will appear whether a search engine user is looking for "Screensavers," "screen savers," "Screen Savers," or
"screensavers."

Some search engines will scan and record these entire lists, and
some will pick up only the first 200, 500 or 1000 characters of each
one; search engines practices not only vary, but also often change,
so there is no way of accommodating them all short of making special pages to attract each one of the majors, and keeping those
pages up to date would take almost constant study of search engine
behavior. You probably wouldn't get enough additional responses
for that amount of effort to be worthwhile, so don't bother with it.
Stick with the "one size fits all" solution.

Note that the DaveCentral keywords repeat themselves a number of times. This artificially increases the word relevancy for many
of the words which the person who drew up this list felt that someone searching for downloadable shareware or free software might
use. Some search engines use all of those keywords, some don't.
But DaveCentral gets over 100,000 pageviews per day without any
paid promotion at all, so this tactic—combined with the fact that
DaveCentral really does have all the content listed in those
metatags—makes it rank high in appropriate searches.

Paid search engine listings are another matter. Some pageview
"bids" on *Overture.com* go over a dollar. Most of the pages that
have these inflated amounts shown sell high-margin products or
services in extremely competitive markets. It is possible that a

company willing to pay a dollar or more just to get someone to look at its site may do this only for a week or two or possibly even just a few days. Perhaps a life insurance sales lead is worth that much, and some catalog merchants who rely on direct mail for most of their new customers might justify the expense by pointing out that it costs more than a dollar to print and mail even a small, simple catalog that includes an order form. The idea of paying for search results should be approached carefully, and you must choose the search words for which you are willing to pay with extreme caution. If you are an insurance agent catering to local individuals in Birmingham, Alabama, or Birmingham, England, you must make sure that you are paying for leads only in or near the correct Birmingham, and you certainly don't want to pay to bring curious eyes in Los Angeles or Tokyo to your Web site.

This goes back to the concept of forgetting about the hundreds of millions of Internet users out there and concentrating only on those who might be interested in your offering, and remembering that this might be only a few thousand people. It also brings up another thought: The amount of good a site listing in a huge, worldwide directory can do you may not be as great as you may think. How many of the millions who hit Yahoo! every day are going to be searching, instead of using Yahoo!'s free Web mail services? And of those searching, how many will be searching for your site or one like it?

Listings in small, regional business directories or, better yet, industry-specific directories, may be at least as productive as listings in major search engines. Whether or not you should pay for listings in regional or industry directories is another question, and you can answer only it by researching directories that cover your industry. Some business areas have excellent ones, and some don't. Some may have many competing directories, all vying for listing dollars and readers' attention. An example of this is the wedding services business. There seem to be hundreds of online directories trying to get florists, photographers, disk jockeys, caterers, limousine operators, and others to pay $10 or more for a listing. The problem is that it would cost hundreds of dollars per month to list in all of them, and most of them have minuscule readerships. Not only that, but there are many wedding services directories that offer free listings, and these directories usually have far more listings, and are therefore more popular, than ones that boast about how, for a small fee, your business can be the "exclusive" listing for your region.

When Paying for Search Engine Leads Makes Good Business Sense

Some companies, especially those in high-markup businesses that rely on their Web sites for sales, may find paid search engine placement worthwhile. Here are three reasons to pay for search engine placement.

1. It obviously works. You see the same companies running paid search engine listings month after month, year after year. These companies are not run by fools. If they didn't feel they were getting their money's worth, they would stop paying for those links.

2. The most expensive paid search engine link costs less than the cheapest TV or print ad when you figure the expense *per qualified prospect* rather than the gross cost per viewer or reader. This is the most tightly focused type of ad campaign you can possibly run. Remember, when you pay for search engine listings, you are running paid advertising, and you must look at those listings as ads, not as *Web content*. An ad is an ad, in any medium.

3. Paid search engine referrals are easy to *turn on* and *turn off*. If you want more leads, you pay for them. If you have enough, you stop paying. You can also test your copy and the keywords you use for very short periods of time and use the increase or decrease in traffic you see to your Web site over a span as short as a few hours to fine-tune your campaign, instead of waiting days or weeks to evaluate each change, as you would need to do in any other medium.

This line of reasoning may not work for a news Web site that may only get a few dollars in advertising revenue per thousand pageviews. But, for a real estate agency or other business that can come up with a defined, closely targeted set of keywords potential customers are likely to use when searching, and stands to make hundreds or thousands of dollars from a single sale, it is a worthwhile promotional tactic.

The problem with directories that offer exclusive listings to businesses is that, by definition, they offer readers a limited set of choices. Readers—your prospects—are less likely to turn to a directory that is obviously no more than a series of paid ads than to one where they can find a larger selection.

None of this has anything to do with technology. It is all about human behavior. Is being a big fish in a small (directory) pond better than being a small fish in a huge search engine ocean? This question takes business-specific research and creative thought to answer, whether you are talking about online directories or paper ones. Once again, the Internet shows itself to be merely a means, not an end in itself.

More Advanced Search Engine Tricks

Beyond the basics mentioned above, "link relevance" has recently become an important factor in the way search engines decide which sites to show readers first in response to keyword-based searches. Up-and-comer Google, especially, uses the number of sites that link to yours as a measure of its popularity. This tends to give preference to seniority; a site that has been online continuously under the same domain name for five years is obviously going to have more outside sites link to it than one that was put up last month, even if the new site is superior in content and layout. This link popularity makes it hard for a new site to get attention, but it also protects searchers from sites that come and go, and helps stabilize the World Wide Web in general. But there is a way to "cheat" this system—or at least to give your new site an even chance against older, better-known online brands

This is where programs and services that claim to submit your site to thousands of search engines or make some similar boast can be useful. Now, there aren't 20,000 true Web search engines. There may be that many directories, possibly more, but most of them are tiny and won't do you any good. Worse, many of the "directory" sites to which most of the automatic submission systems will submit your site are "Free For All" (FFA) links sites that post submitted links in random order. These sites are not really used by anyone who wants to find product or services on the World Wide Web. Almost all of them are run by low-end promoters who use them to gather lists of "opportunity seekers" or "Internet marketers" they can sell to yet other "opportunity seekers" as "opt-in, targeted email lists" to which large quantities of spam can be sent.

The only reason to bother with this shady side of the Internet is that getting lots of links to your site on many other sites, even crummy sites, makes your site look popular, and this can help it rise to the top on search engine and directory pages that use link popularity as one of their selection criteria.

But before you play the FFA game, get a "throwaway" email address, one you will never use for anything but site submissions, and make sure that is the one that goes in all the "your email address" forms in the submissions software, any submission service's Web page, or directly into any form on a directory site you are not absolutely sure is on the up-and-up and will not abuse your contact information.

Now get one of the "submit to thousands of search engines and directories" programs or sign up with one of the services that does this, make sure you disable submissions to the major search engines from which you may get substantial numbers of qualified readers, and submit away.

Another good way to improve search engine placement is to have, and submit, multiple domains; that is, to have "sections" of your site that all have their own sets of metatags and their own content. This is both easy and legitimate, although on some hosting services' lower-cost plans it may cost extra. The trick is, instead of having your site sections filed in the traditional manner, like this:

BigBusiness.com/ (home page)
BigBusiness.com/products
BigBusiness.com/about
BigBusiness.com/press
BigBusiness.com/news
BigBusiness.com/contact

. . . and so on, do it this way:

BigBusiness.com/ (home page)
Products.BigBusiness.com
About.BigBusiness.com
Press.BigBusiness.com
News.BigBusiness.com
Contact.BigBusiness.com

Now you have six separate domain names, at least the way many search engines define a "domain," even though you have only one registered domain name.

You can give each of these "Third Level Domains," as they are called in the trade, a little extra search engine oomph by giving each one its own set of metatags that reflects its own content instead of using a single generic set of tags for all of your site's pages.

Advertising Your Web Site Online

The basic online advertising unit since the World Wide Web opened up to commercial use has been the top-of-the-page banner ad. This is still the most popular form of Web site advertising, but there are now many alternatives to this old standard, and more are coming.

One of the best recent online advertising values to appear is Google's keyword-linked text ads. They are obviously not part of the search results, as shown in Figure 7–1, so Google users are not being flummoxed, but they are in character with the rest of the

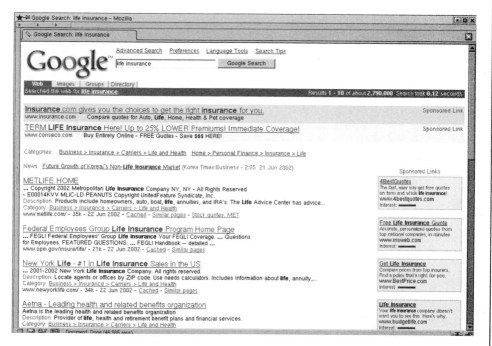

■ **Figure 7–1 A Google search for "life insurance" brings up many keyword-triggered text ads on the right side of the page.**

site's content; that is, they are not a blinking or jumping graphic stuck in an out-of-the-way location on the page that readers can easily ignore, but are right next to the search results, where a Google user is most likely to glance at them.

Other Web sites are running large graphical ads in the middle of their pages, and these ads were generating response rates four to five times higher than top-of-the-page banners in the early months of 2002.

The best place to keep up with the latest trends in online advertising is the Interactive Advertising Bureau (IAB) Web site at *www.iab.net.* IAB members all have a vested interest in the success of online advertising, and their content tends to be slanted toward large businesses, but it is good to look at their ever-changing content before making any advertising decisions of your own.

Don't be afraid to experiment. Try a few text ads, try different banner ad sizes, try running ads on different sites, and track all your results carefully. Then—and this is so basic that it shouldn't need to be said, but it is a rule that is often ignored by companies of all sizes—spend more on what works, and less on what doesn't. Your advertising program should constantly evolve as you come up with new ideas, and some of them work and others fail. The statistical homework needed to track ad results is boring in the extreme, but it is absolutely necessary to keep costs low and results high.

Take the traditional PR route. If you are selling products or services online, find news Web sites that cover your business area. Send press releases to them. Make sure you send releases only to those that either cover your industry or geographic region; others are not going to be interested, and will consider inappropriate press releases spam. On the other hand, online news editors who do cover your area will generally be enthusiastic about your information. Gathering news is expensive and tedious, and competition among news Web sites is fierce. Well-written, relevant press releases sent to online media have an excellent chance of being turned into stories.

Advertising Your Web Site Offline

The most obvious place to advertise your Web site is in literature you already use every day: your business cards, stationery, and printed brochures. Adding your Web address to them is no big deal. Indeed, it is becoming such a normal part of printed business material these days that its absence will probably be more noticed than its inclusion.

Sometimes Cooperation Is the Best Promotion

If you have a small or new business, you are going to have to display a little more imagination than the big companies IAB's information is aimed at. Here are some ideas for promotion using online advertising that cost almost nothing:

- Find other online business people who sell to the same customers you do, but don't sell competitive products, and exchange links or ad banners with them. There are a number of formal exchanges that do this sort of thing, but they generally limit their exchanges to banner ads only, and about half the banners they run on your site will not be cross-promoters, just plain ad banners unrelated to your business. This is how the banner exchange companies earn their money. You can much better on your own job if you're willing to do your own research and make direct contact with non-competitive merchants or information providers to set up your own swap arrangements—and if you make your own deals you won't be limited to ad banners, but can work with text links, mutual testimonials, and whatever else you and your swap partners dream up together.

- If your primary "product" is news or information, content sharing arrangements can help boost traffic. NewsForge (*www.newsforge.com*) has agreements with the U.K.-based online IT publication, *The Register* (*www.theregister.co.uk*), and with NewsFactor Networks (*www.newsfactor.com*), neither of which competes directly with NewsForge's concentration on Linux and Open Source software news, but goes for more general information technology audiences. Competition is good, but so is cooperation. For niche-oriented news sites, especially, a chance to broaden coverage at little or no cost is a bonus over and above readership gains that content sharing can produce. The original, pre-commercial Internet was built on cooperation. It's still a good idea—and not only online, either.

The next phase is to add your URL to all your advertising. Whether you're a solo entrepreneur or an executive working for a world-wide corporate empire, you need to make sure that as many potential customers as possible see your Web site, because it is the least expensive, easiest-to-update piece of customer contact material you can possibly have, so the more people you can get to go to your Web site, then bookmark it and return to it over and over, the more effective a sales tool it will become. But this should not be a one-way street. If you run regional newspaper inserts or run one-store specials, your Web site should point back to these specials, and should even suggest buying the newspapers where you consistently run sale ads, because customers can easily carry your paper-printed sales notices into the store with them, while they are unlikely to carry their computers when they go shopping.

Yes, you can (and should) include online coupons on your Web site that customers can print out and take with them, but you should also use your Web site to help boost your offline promotions whenever possible, just as TV station Web sites put their schedules online to help boost viewership. This goes right back to the basic philosophy of using your Web site as a business tool, rather than looking at your Web site as a business in and of itself.

But your Web site is a *valuable* business tool, and drumming its address into customers' heads is worthwhile. That address should be on the sides of your trucks, if you own trucks. It should be at the bottom of the screen during the entire run time of all your TV ads. It should be in every print ad you run, perhaps placed more prominently than the lower right hand corner, where it often ends up in ads run by companies that haven't yet learned how to use the Internet effectively. That Web address—that URL, that domain name—is as valuable as a storefront sign on a busy commercial street, and you must not only choose it as carefully as you would choose a retail location, but you must make sure it is as easy to find as a store you own.

Choosing the Right Domain Name

Here's yet another situation where the World-Wideness of the Internet becomes a disadvantage rather than an advantage. In the old days, you could have local businesses named "Joe's Appliance" in every state and every country, all listed in local business directories, and no one cared or got them confused. Now *joesappliance.com* is a single, worldwide name. Only one business can have it. Once there's a *joesappliance.com* in Auckland, New Zealand, there can't be another one in Los Angeles, California, or Pretoria, South Africa.

The best solution to this problem is more use of "country codes" like .uk (United Kingdom), .za (South Africa), and .us (United States). The U.S. hopes to break the .us top-level domain down further by states, using the common post office two-letter abbreviations for them, so you could have a *joesappliancea.ca.us* in California and a *joesappliances.ny.us* in New York. But for the moment, .com is king of the commercial Internet in customers' minds, so we need to be creative.

Joes-appliances.com is obvious, but will customers remember it or will they be confused? Joes_appliances has the same problem; "-" and "_" are about the only punctuation marks allowed in domain names (apostrophes aren't, which is why the original one wasn't "joe'sappliances.com") so there is little chance to get clever that way. You can't use capitalization, since upper case and lower case don't matter in domain names; to the "root servers" that translate human-readable domain names into IP (Internet Protocol) numerical addresses like 131.103.237.139, JoesAppliances and joesappliances are exactly the same.

You may want to try using your physical location as part of your domain name if the one you'd prefer is already taken. *JoesOfLosAngeles.com* may not be as elegant as you'd like, but chances are it's still available for you, and if it's not, something like *Joe'sLAappliance.com*, *JoesApplianceLA.com* or some other useful combination *will* be.

Make a list of possible names. Incorporate your business's name or some part of it if at all possible. Come up with a few others that don't use your business name, too. Shorter is better, but chances are you are going to have a minimum of 10 letters these days; most domain names shorter than that are taken.

The next step is to go to one of the domain name registries (use Google and the search words "domain registry" to find them) and try out your favorite name selections to see which ones, if any, are available. Note the "ones" instead of "one"—you can have more than one domain name for your site, possibly one long one, like JoesAppliancesOfLosAngeles, and one shorter, catchier one, like JoesWashers.

Now register the name or names you have chosen, following the domain registrar's instructions (they're all easy), but first, please check this bold-type warning:

Get the spelling right!

Domain name registration is an automated process, and the computers that handle it will accept JoesAppliances just as happily as they will accept JoesAppliances. This is not a place to make mistakes that will embarrass you later. Domain name selection and registration are two of the most critical parts of your Internet business presence, and deserve plenty of thought and care at every step.

There is one last, increasingly imporant, but typically overlooked factor in selecting a domain name: Make sure it doesn't infringe on someone else's copyright or trademark. Five years ago lawsuits over domain names were rare. Now they've become common. Just because a domain name isn't registered doesn't mean it doesn't infringe on someone's copyright. Imagine registering *FastEZPlumbing.com* as the online sales channel for your new line of snap-together water inlet fittings, building that domain name and sales from your site to a respectable level, and then, one morning, you receive a letter from a law firm representing Fast EZ Plumbing Fixtures, Inc., saying that you are infringing upon their trademark, which they've held since 1958. Fast EZ Plumbing Fixtures, Inc., wants you to give your domain name to them, because it's really theirs, thank you very much.

What now? Run up a big legal bill trying to keep "your" name? Change your domain name and hope all your customers find the new one? Either choice will be expensive. The best course of action, if you find yourself in this situation, is to try to work out some accomodation with the other party. Perhaps you turn over your domain to them, but in return they place a prominent link to your new one on the main page of their site. Or perhaps you help them find a similar domain name, like *Fast-EZ-Plumbing.com*, and your two companies exchange links so that both of your Web presences are multiplied.

Or you can try to avoid this kind of problem before it happens, by checking trademark registries before you invest promotional effort into a domain name. You can do this research online. In the U.S., the Patent and Trademark Office's URL is *www.uspto.gov*. In the U.K., go to *www.patent.gov.uk*. Almost every country has something similar. You should check with an attorney wherever you are, since trademark laws vary from country to country, and even in the U.K. and U.S. they can be fuzzy and hard to understand.

Protecting Your Domain Name

This is the flip side of the domain name dispute problem. If you are successful with your online operation, sooner or later someone is going to try to use a name similar to yours, either on purpose or by mistake. Now you must decide what action to take, if any.

In general, being nice is the best tactic. If the name overlap is an honest one from a legitimate business run by decent people, the best thing you can do is make sure both your sites carry prominent links to the other's, be friends, and go on about your business. The legal cost of this kind of arrangement is zero if you can do it with an informal contract, and very low even if you decide on a negotiated contract that specifies link and logo size, and its exact placement on each business's site.

Doing nothing at all can also be a good decision in many cases. If your site's content and <metatags> are clear, in most cases there is little chance of customers confusing the two businesses even if their real-life names and domain names are similar, as long as they are located in different places or don't compete directly with each other.

A far more nefarious situation is the porn peddler or other unsavory business person who intentionally gets a domain name a single letter or other easily-made mistake away from a popular site's domain name in order to draw "typo traffic." The most famous example of this is *www.whitehouse.com*; as of March, 2002, it was still there, still claiming, "We are the Worldwide Leader in Adult and Political Entertainment . . ."

This site has been around since 1997, getting traffic because many people looking for the United States President's site type ".com" instead of the correct "*www.whitehouse.gov*" address. If your site draws significant traffic or is attached to a heavily promoted brand name, you may want to spend some time, now and then, typing in domain names similar to yours to see what you find. If they're pornographers, spammers, or others whose business practices don't jive with your standards, you may be able to resolve the problem through ICANN (_www.icann.org_), the Internet Corporation for Assigned Names and Numbers. This body controls domain name assignments. There have been many complaints about how it handles domain name disputes, but it is the only mechanism currently available worldwide.

The other alternative is the court system wherever you are, and if you are dealing with someone in another country whom you believe is misusing your domain name in some way, there are jurisdiction problems even though most countries have signed intellectual property rights treaties that are supposed to help make trademark and copyright laws uniform throughout the world, especially as they apply to Internet matters.

Try Not to Argue Over Domain Names

In general, unless another domain name clearly and obviously interferes with your ability to operate in a clear and reputable manner online, it is best to avoid disputes, especially if your company is large and the alleged infringer is an individual or a small company. Even if you are "right," you don't want headlines about how you try to push small fry around; if your company's name is "Whittlesonmeyer's" and an individual whose name is also "Whittlesonmeyer" has already registered "Whittlesonmeyer" as a domain name, he or she has just as much right to it as you. Perhaps you can buy the name from the current holder or make some other amicable arrangement to use it. Your best approach is obviously personal and courteous, with no mention of attorneys or legal action, because, as you know all too well, many people interpret threats as calls to battle and are unwilling to deal with anyone who has previously shown hostility toward them.

Lawsuits against "parody" site names like "_yourcompany-sucks.com_" are thrown out by U.S. courts at least as often as they are upheld, and the "yourcompany" people almost always get reams of bad publicity—and bring lots of attention to the "sucks" site—in the process.

Win or lose, domain name disputes, lawsuits, and lawsuit threats are often at least as harmful to the company that initiates them as they are to their targets.

All Your Promotions Must Work Together

Okay, you have a great domain name that accurately reflects your business's name and location, one that will stick easily in customers' minds. You have developed clever online cross-promotions with other Web site owners, and have made wise online advertising decisions. You have your domain name on your letterheads, your business cards, in your print ads and telephone directory listings, in any TV spots you run, possibly even on your signs if you have visible retail locations.

But things need to go in the other direction, too. Your Web site should tell potential customers that you are listed in phone directories—and which ones—in case a potential customer is trying to find your business and does not have a computer handy. Retail locations should be shown on your Web site, and maps showing how to find those locations should be available for those who need them, not shoved in every site user's face, but as a "click here for directions" link to a separate page in accordance with the information layering principle you have used as the basis of your site structure.

If you have a sales flier running in the upcoming edition of a local newspaper, your Web site should steer people to it, just as the sales flier should steer customers to your Web site.

All promotional devices you use, including your Web site, should work together. Cross-fertilization can and should enhance them all.

Cost Control and Futureproofing

The 20th century stereotype of an Internet company included images of company-paid massages, corporate headquarters with free recreational facilities, programmers bringing their dogs to work, everyone from the CEO on down dressed in t-shirts and sandals, fancy designer office chairs and desks, and the most expensive possible desktop and laptop computer for every employee. Naturally, all of this ostentation, and the server computers behind it, had to be located in Silicon Valley or San Francisco, Manhattan, Boston or its suburbs, the most expensive parts of London, or another location where living expenses were guaranteed to be among the world's highest.

Comfortable chairs are nice, but there is no reason for people who work on the Internet to have special chairs or desks or computers that are different from those used in any other business. A Web graphics designer needs the same amount of computer power as a graphics designer who works on newspaper ads—and the "print" designer probably uses the Internet nearly as often as the Web designer these days.

The idea that salaries for people who work on the Internet should be higher than those paid to people who do similar work in other media has also gone away. A reporter or editor who has well-developed Internet research skills should be just as valuable to a newspaper or magazine as to an online publisher. For a while it seemed like everyone in the newspaper business this side of the big national papers like *The New York Times* or *The Guardian* was drifting onto the Internet and making twice as much money. Now we are starting to see saner salary levels for online writers, who can command a premium only if they offer technical skills beyond basic reporting and writing ability—but they ought to command a premium for these same skills from print and broadcast media employers too.

Employer complaints about Java or Active-X programmers with only a year or two of experience demanding starting salaries equivalent to those dished out to experienced corporate auditors or factory managers seem to have abated. There is no longer any need to pay extra money to someone just because he or she is working on the Internet. As in any field, employees whom you treat fairly will do better work than those who feel they are not being treated well, but there is no need to treat Internet people as special or give them leeway beyond what you extend to other creative employees.

A Distributed Work Force Saves Money

The Internet breaks down geographic barriers on the sales side. We've talked about this in previous chapters, and it's not a new idea. But what is new—or at least not yet widespread—is using the Internet to hire and manage employees and freelancers in remote locations.

Consider a magazine editorial and production staff as an example. More often than not, reporters and editors in offices a few feet away from each other now communicate by email, and layout and graphics people send graphics files back and forth to each other over the company's computer network. The next stage is to ask, "If these people use the company's own network as their primary means of communication, why not take that one step further, and stop caring whether everyone is in the same building or even in the same city?" "Cracking the whip" to make sure a graphics artist is at his or her desk is not necessary; they're logged and working or not no matter where they are. The same is true of programmers, and writers and editors have been working with each other long-distance for many years. (In fact, this book is being written in Florida and edited in Texas, even though the publisher is located in New

Jersey. This book is not only about the Internet, but is being *created over* the Internet.)

Web site design work is a natural for outsourcing from high-cost areas to low-cost areas. Most of the actual labor involved in putting together a large Web site is tedious coding that requires no personal contact between the person doing it and the client whose site is being worked on. As long as they have a way to communicate, and the client has a way to rapidly view and approve design work, and an easy way to note desired changes and transmit them back to the designer, distance doesn't matter.

Email, with page proofs sent as attachments, can serve as the communications medium for a project in its early stages, when site architecture and page layouts are still being determined. A bit later, when these basics have been handled, it is simple to put the site on a server that requires password access so that the site's navigation scheme and other functions can be tested and changed as needed. (Any competent Web designer can easily set up a private server; you should be suspicious of one who can't.)

This pattern of communication is already common in the Web design industry, even when everyone involved in making a new site is in the same building. Why shouldn't an innovative, cost-cutting Internet maven like you take it to the next step, and use the Internet to find a talented designer in Kentucky or Scotland or some other place where costs are lower than in major business centers? It's probably wise to stay within your own culture and country for Web design and copywriting, since it is easy to make unintentional mistakes about another culture's likes and dislikes even without bringing language barriers into the mix. But within your country, there is no reason not to work with people who are in areas where business costs are low and competition for jobs is high.

Hiring programmers from far away is another matter. Here it may pay to go international, although language and time-zone problems can easily eat up any savings in hourly costs. Many U.S. firms have taken to subcontracting routine programming tasks to Indian companies that charge as little as one-fifth as much as their U.S. competitors. This pattern has worked for some and has not worked for others. The problem with both design and programming work is that they are essentially creative endeavors, not assembly-line work, so there must be a certain amount of "meeting of the minds" between you and the person or persons you hire to perform these tasks for you.

The question, "How do I find these people if they're not near me?" has an easy answer: "Use the Internet." On the simplest and most basic level, while you are looking at other sites, deciding what features you do and don't like before you build your own, you are going to run across at least a few that trigger a nearly instinctive, "Hey, I really like the way this looks" reaction. Almost all freelance Web designers sign their work with a small link to their company's URL at the bottom of each client's main page. If you see a site you like, make a note of the designer and contact him or her. If you don't see a way to contact the designer, it takes only a second to dash off a, "Nice site—who made it? I'm making my own site soon and might like to hire them!" email to _webmaster@ReallyNiceSite.com_ or any another contact email you see on the site you admire. Even if the designer is a staff employee of the company that owns the site you like, as is often the case, he or she may be willing to work for you freelance on the side. There's no harm in asking, certainly, and if the answer is "No," you have still given out a well-deserved compliment. And since Web designers rarely live or work in a vacuum (they have professional associations—like almost everyone else), a Web designer whose work you admire probably can point you to others with similar levels of skill and talent.

Selecting programmers is trickier if you are not a programmer yourself. If you are, you can (and should) ask for code samples and review them, and make your decision based on what you see. Otherwise, you are probably better off leaving the choice of a programmer up to the designer. He or she almost certainly has a working relationship with at least one programmer, and once again that intangible meeting of the minds factor comes into play; if you hire a designer who turns to a programmer of his or her choice (and whose work you can view online and, even as a "mere user," determine if all the links and other basic functions work correctly), you are getting a team that is likely to work together more smoothly and be more productive than if you throw two strangers together and hope their end product is to your liking.

Again, where the parties live and work is not important. Across town, across the country, it's all really the same—at least on the Internet. By expanding the geographic range of your search you suddenly increase your options many-fold. Not only that—and this is true especially if you live in a "tech center" region— you cut down your chance of getting a site that looks similar to those designed by other locals. Web designers, like members of all other trades and professions, tend to form groups and meet, and often copy each other's style even if they do it subconsciously.

Cost-Effective Web Hosting

In mid-2002, the minimum cost of a reliable, business-capable Web hosting service in the U.S. was around $16 per month. You could get a business Web site hosted for less, even for free, if you were willing to accept a stack of restrictions and possibly some huge, unexpected charges if your site got too popular.

Hardly anything has changed since then. Contracts written by Web hosting services are still full of loopholes that allow them to charge you extra if you have an unexpected burst of site visitors, let them turn your site off (possibly without a refund) if anyone complains in any way about any material on your site or about email you send out that mentions your domain name, and do other things to you that might make you very angry. And, naturally, most of these contracts contain anti-lawsuit provisions of one sort or another or require you to file suit—or answer a lawsuit which the hosting service files against you—in a jurisdiction far from your home or office. Worse yet, no matter how vital your Web site may be to your business, you will find that virtually all Web hosting services, no matter how loudly they may boast about their reliability in their sales material, bury some sort of clause in their contracts that say they are responsible for reimbursing you only for whatever fee you have paid them, pro-rated to cover only the outage time, and that they are not liable for any other losses you suffer as a result of your Web site being unreachable by the public.

Reading Web hosting service contracts can be as depressing as reading the End User License Agreements (EULAs) that cover any commercial software you use, and if you are like most people, you have blindly clicked "I agree" many times without reading what responsibility commercial software vendors take for their products' behavior (usually none) and the restrictions that software licenses place upon you as a user (often major, even onerous ones). For some reason, even seasoned executives who would never sign a building lease without going over it line by line, possibly with help from an attorney, often accept software and Web hosting contracts without even skimming through them.

In Web hosting contracts, the single most important clause, for most commercial customers, deals with how much bandwidth your site is allowed. A dialup ISP that advertises unlimited access can safely assume that no customer will be online more than 168 hours per week, because that's how many hours there are in a week. A

Web site's potential bandwidth use is far more open-ended than this, which is why ISPs and Web hosts are more likely to place bandwidth limits on Web sites than on dialup connections. Assume that a simple Web page consists of a 20-Kilobyte (KB) HTML file, and two 40-K image files. Each time a user reads this page, 100 KB of information are sent from the server to the user's computer. Our example site gets an average of 1000 readers per month, so its normal monthly bandwidth usage is around 100,000 KB, or 100 Megabytes (MB), per month. This is well within the bandwidth allotment that most Web hosting services allow in their lowest-cost hosting packages. (It is also all the traffic a restaurant or other local business needs to get on its Web site to make it a better marketing value than print ads or telephone directory listings.) Now imagine a disaster: Horror of horrors, this humble little site suddenly wins a design award of some sort or is selected for inclusion in a "Best of the Web" directory or otherwise achieves sudden popularity. Suddenly 100,000 people want to look at it every day. 100,000 viewers times 100 KB per pageview equals 10 Megabytes of bandwidth every day. If this site is hosted under a contract that allows 100 MB of data transfer per month—which seemed like more than enough when the site's owner made his or her hosting arrangements—it is now going to use up all of its allotment in 10 days.

Now what?

This depends on the specific Web host's contract terms. Some will continue serving pages and charge for excess bandwidth use. These charges can easily run into hundreds of dollars. Some hosting services will place a clamp on bandwidth use if your site is suddenly hit hard. This means that not everyone trying to view your site is going to get through to see it or that it will load very slowly for most users during peak load periods. Yet other hosting services simply stop serving your pages when you reach your bandwidth limits. In effect, once you use up your allotment, they take your site off the Internet.

Even a small, simple site that expects only modest traffic should have a minimum capacity of 5000 MB (5 GB) per month. You can easily get this much or more for between $20 and $25 per month base fee, and additional charges of $8 to $10 per additional Gigabyte are generally considered reasonable in the retail hosting industry, although some hosting services may try to charge you anywhere between $15 and $50 per additional Gigabyte of data transfer. *Read that contract before you sign it! This stuff is all in there!*

Six Degrees of Web Hosting Service

Depending on your needs, you may be able to spend less than $20 per month to host your Web site—or you may need to spend millions per year. There are six major hosting service classifications. The dividing lines between them are not clear-cut and they change constantly, but this will give you a general idea of what to expect from—and what to pay for—different levels of Web hosting.

Shared Hosting

This is the most basic, lowest-cost way to put a simple Web site on the Internet. The files that make up your site are stored on a server computer's hard drive that also contains files for many other Web sites. You have a password that controls access to the section of the hard drive that contains your files, but you cannot access other files on the server. Conversely, other site owners cannot access your files. Basic shared hosting charges can range from free (with other companies' ads appearing on your pages; this makes you look like a clueless amateur, so don't bite on the "free hosting" deals, okay?) to about $100 per month. Most shared hosting plans in the $20 to $30 per month range offer enough server space and file transfer capacity—also called bandwidth—to accommodate a small business's needs unless that business has a database-driven Web site made up of hundreds of pages and pictures.

Ecommerce Hosting

This is an evolving specialty in the Web hosting business: shared hosting that includes built-in ecommerce facilities like merchant accounts and templates to create "instant" catalog pages, "shopping carts," and "checkouts" with your logo on them. Many ecommerce hosts will either help you set up a credit card merchant account or have arrangements that allow you to share theirs—for a fee. Expect to pay $100 to $400 in setup fees, including merchant account startup, although many ecommerce hosts offer periodic "no start fees" specials. Expect to pay hosting fees ranging from $35 to $200 per month, plus credit card processing fees that are 1% to 2% higher than offline merchants pay. Ecommerce hosts that derive some of their income from credit card processing are likely to have less strict bandwidth limits than those that don't. While not always the cheapest way to put a direct sales site online, ecommerce hosting is usually the easiest and least time-consuming, and the hosting service takes responsibility for keeping transactions—and your customers' credit card numbers—secure, which makes it "the" choice for small business people who do not have Web security experience themselves or access to anyone who does.

Dedicated Hosting

You lease an entire server computer from the hosting service, including space for it on their premises and use of their bandwidth up to a set limit, plus fees for extra bandwidth above that limit. You or an employee or subcontractor can configure "your" server remotely with any software you want; usually Linux and Apache are the most efficient and cost-effective choices, but whatever you choose, you are responsible for it. Security and software reliability are up to you, not to the hosting service. Prices for dedicated hosting generally start around $100 per month for a single server computer capable of operating a modest ecommerce or news/information site that gets fewer than 10,000 daily pageviews, and can range into thousands per month for more powerful (or multiple) servers that can handle traffic loads of up to 500,000 pageviews per day. Do not even think about dedicated hosting unless you know how to administer and secure a Web server or are willing to hire someone who does. This is strictly an expert's game.

Managed Hosting

This is essentially dedicated hosting with the hosting service providing the systems expertise and labor. Base prices can start out as low as $150 per month for Linux servers, and around $200 per month for Windows servers, but at this level you can expect to pay extra almost every time one of the hosting company's network administrators goes anywhere near your server. More realistically, for full-service managed hosting you can expect to pay $600 per month and up for Linux servers, depending on the specific software you select, and $900 and up for Windows servers. Managed hosting prices are negotiated based on the specific software and services you need. If you are not fully familiar with the art (and it is an art) of setting up and maintaining Web servers, and none of your employees has this expertise, you may want to hire a consultant to help you find, evaluate, and negotiate with managed hosting service suppliers. Although dealing with a managed hosting service takes less day-to-day knowledge (and less of your or your workers' time) than running your own dedicated servers, it still takes a certain amount of knowledge. Managed servers can safely and economically be used up to about the 500,000 pages/day level, beyond which you are probably better off owning your own equipment.

Co-Location Service

You own your own servers and routers. You hire your own network administrators and do your own hardware maintenance. You supply your own software. All the "co-lo" people (as they are called in trade slang) give you is a locked-up space in their facility where you can put your servers, along with a direct, high-speed connection to the Internet, power, air conditioning, physical security, and usually wiring for a phone line or two in the "cage" where your servers are located. Your admins and techs get bathroom keys and access to drink and snack machines and a break room, and they'll need these, because if you are at the million-pageview-per-day point where it starts to make sense to control all your own hardware and hire your own technical staff, your people will be in that co-lo facility almost every day, with one of your admins on call nearby or even in the building twenty-four hours a day, seven days a week, just in case something goes wrong. Co-lo is strictly for the "big boys and girls" on the

Internet for whom combined hardware, bandwidth, and labor expenses run into hundreds of thousands of dollars—or more—annually. (You know who you are.)

Do-It-Yourself Hosting

You have DSL or other high-speed Internet access at your home or office, a spare computer, and a set of Linux CDs, so you decide to set up your own server. You'll have total control of everything, but you will also have responsibility for everything. If your electricity goes out and you don't have a backup power source, your site will go offline. If your server's hard drive dies in the middle of the night, do you want to get up and replace it? Or are you going to have a backup server and automatic failover? What if your Internet connection fails? Once again, your site is down.

Small-scale, do-it-yourself hosting is for computer hobbyists and students, not serious business people. The only rational reason to run a Web server in your home or office is to learn how to do it. This is not bad knowledge to have, whether you are a solo Internet entrepreneur or president of a company that has an extensive online operation, but chances are that a site hosted by a professional hosting service that has redundant Internet connections in case one dies, backup hardware to plug in at a moment's notice, and a backup generator out back in case of an extended power failure, can keep your site up and running more reliably than you can on your own.

At the top end of the hosting scale, you may be better off running your own servers than renting space in a co-lo facility. It is entirely possible that you can save measurable sums of money, without sacrificing reliability, by building your own hosting facility in a low-cost industrial park building in an area where sysadmins don't command top-level salaries. Naturally, you need multiple backbone connections and your own backup power generators, and all employees who work in your server facility must be trained to keep doors locked, and admit only fellow employees or known visitors.

Where you put this facility doesn't really matter, as long as it has the required Internet access, plus reliable electricity and phone service. If you're in Boston and you want an excuse to go fishing on the Florida Golf Coast frequently, put it there. If you're an avid ice fisherman headquartered in San Francisco, put your servers in Minnesota. A golfer in London might choose a town in Scotland, and so on. You may even end up with an entire satellite operation in your low-cost secondary location, built around your server facility, that provides workspace for some of your writers, editors, designers, programmers and clerical workers who can all live and work there for less than they would need in a high-cost business center—and that means even more savings.

It is easy to be seduced by Web hosting services that advertise rates of $10 per month or even less, but taking these offers is generally not a good idea. You want your site hosted by a company that has backup servers which they can throw into service immediately if one of their primaries fails, has backup power supplies that can keep them online in case of thunderstorms or other problems, has redundant connections to the "Internet backbone" in case one fails for any reason, and has a skilled staff that can protect your site from hackers and "denial of service" attacks (where hackers use automated tools to overwhelm a server's capacity by requesting thousands of pages per second so that legitimate users can't get through). All of this costs money and requires a certain amount of organizational heft to maintain. There is a price point below which no company can afford to offer truly reliable Web hosting service, and it is foolish to try to shop below that price point.

Save Money with Open Source Software

Managed hosting suppliers typically charge much less to maintain servers that run the Linux operating system and Apache server software than they charge to maintain servers running Windows and Microsoft IIS server software. These people are professionals in a competitive business who look at each nickel they spend. If they charge less to maintain servers running Open Source software than to maintain servers running proprietary software like Windows and IIS, it's because they have made careful cost and reliability comparisons and have decided that Linux and Apache are more efficient than the alternatives.

Linux

Linux is generally the best operating system choice for Web servers. License cost is zero, and sysadmins with strong Linux skills are easy to find. Many leading-edge techies use Linux not only as a server operating system, but also to run their home desktops and home networks for the same reasons that it is the fastest-growing Web server operating system:

- Virus resistance—Linux is not affected by any of the common Windows-borne viruses or worms that infest the Internet.
- Reliability—Linux servers can (and often do) run for years without rebooting.
- Hardware savings—Linux can (and does) run well on simple, inexpensive, even obsolete hardware.
- Flexibility—You can modify Linux any way you want. If, for example, you are going to run a server farm where you are going to use uniform hardware, you can create a "stripped" version of Linux that contains only the functions and device drivers needed to operate your specific hardware. This saves hard drive space and speeds processing time.
- Compatibility—Linux runs on everything from handheld (PDA) computers to IBM mainframes, and on both Mac and "Wintel" computers.

- Software availability—There are many Linux programs that sysadmins can use to "tweak" system performance, monitor network integrity, detect and thwart intrusion attempts, balance loads between servers, and even group computers together in clusters to handle large tasks. Almost all major database and ERP (Enterprise Resource Planning) software packages are available for Linux, and there are Linux software packages that enable interoperability with Windows, while there is very little Windows software available that ensures interoperability with Linux or any other non-Windows operating system at the server level.

- Rapid development and bug fixing—Security holes and other bugs found in Linux and Open Source programs are typically fixed within hours and are shared freely across the Internet.

The major concern which corporate managers seem to have about Linux is lack of a central company behind it to offer support and accept liability for any failures. This is a bit of a head-scratcher for Linux users who have read the End User License Agreements (EULAs) for proprietary programs, including Windows and most commercial Unix versions, that absolve their publishers of any liability for their products' failures. Support for Linux, just as for any other operating system, is typically handled by contract, either with local firms or larger, even multi-national companies. IBM and Hewlett-Packard, for example, provide dedicated Linux service and support for most of their server products. Linux distribution publishers like Red Hat, SuSE, MandrakeSoft, and many others provide installation and ongoing maintenance support, plus customization and programming services for the "flavors" of Linux each one produces, and because all the different Linux versions share the same basic technical underpinnings, support for one means support for all. But the biggest secret of commercial Linux support is that you may not need it. If your sysadmins, whether full-time employees or consultants, join any one of many Linux mutual support email lists or IRC channels, they can get all the technical help they need for free. The only payment they are expected to make is to help others in return, and to freely share any modifications they make to Linux or any free software that runs on Linux with the rest of the world, just as others share freely with them.

Linux has long had a reputation as a hard-to-use operating system "for geeks only," but this is no longer true. New point-and-click interfaces have been developed that make Linux very easy to set up and use. But to use all of Linux's power and depth, you still need to know how to use complex text commands—in other words, to be an enterprise-level Linux guru you must be a true computer geek who delights in talking to computers in their own language. There is nothing wrong with this. You *want* hard-core individuals to run your servers, because those same hard-core geeks will love and cherish them, and tweak them for maximum performance, and take pride in keeping them reliable and secure every second of every hour of every day.

There are several Unix variants called FreeBSD, OpenBSD, and NetBSD that share many of Linux's good points (including free use), and actually have several technical advantages over Linux. But Linux has mass acceptance, and the BSDs do not. It is a "betamax vs. VHS" situation. Sometimes it is simply more prudent in a business sense to go with the accepted industry standard, and for high-reliability, low-cost Web servers, that's Linux.

Apache

Apache is the world's most popular Web server. The Apache Software Foundation, located online at *www.apache.org*, is the central body behind Apache server development. The original Apache Project was started in 1995 by a small group of Internet pioneers who wanted better Web server software than was already available. They cobbled together a server program that was, as the legend goes, nothing but "patches," or simple fixes to existing software, and called it "A Patchy Server" in one of those punishing moments that seem to infest the brains of otherwise intelligent and comparatively sane programmers from time to time. New and more advanced versions of Apache have been released steadily ever since.

Apache support is obtainable through channels similar to those that provide Linux support, and a company called Covalent (*www.covalent.net*) has developed a commercial software package that makes managing Apache-based servers easy even for sysadmins who have not worked with Apache before, and streamlines administration of large Apache installations (in other words, *saves labor*) for workers of all skill levels.

Perl vs. PHP vs. Java

These are the three most popular programming languages for Web development. All are available for free, and most Web designers and programmers are familiar with at least one of them. Microsoft has a scripting language called Active-X that is easy to use, but has major security problems, and works completely only for site users running Windows and Microsoft Internet Explorer browser.

Among Perl, PHP, and Java, the choice is hard. Each has strong points and weak points. You might as well just go with whichever one your designer knows best. If you are determined to learn one scripting language yourself, PHP might be your best choice. PHP is an acronym for "Personal Home Page." Anyone, using any browser on any kind of computer, can read almost any Web site coded in PHP.

Stick to Industry Standards

At the time of this writing, Microsoft's Internet Explorer (MSIE) is the dominant Web browser, used by somewhere between 80% and 90% (estimates vary) of all computers hooked to the Internet. Many site owners have looked at this statistic, and have decided to make sites that fully work only with MSIE.

But it is dangerous to tie your Web site's future to any one browser or operating system, even if it comes from a company as seemingly unstoppable as Microsoft. Not many years ago, Netscape was the dominant, apparently unstoppable Web browser company, and Netscape browsers had few things they could do that were not part of the Internet coding and HTML display standards laid down by the World Wide Web Consortium (_W3C.org_). Since the vast majority of Internet users back then—1995 or 1996—used Netscape, many Web designers incorporated Netscape-specific features into their pages. And then, when MSIE started to get popular, they had to redo all their work.

History repeats itself. Now AOL seems to be moving from MSIE toward a custom Internet browser it designed itself, based on the same programming that has gone into recent Netscape and Mozilla browsers. (AOL owns Netscape, so this is a totally logical business move.) AOL, by most estimates, controls about 30% of all

Internet traffic. This means every site that is fully compatible only with MSIE (and that includes most sites made with Microsoft's FrontPage software) must be redesigned or face potentially severe traffic losses.

Netscape is now on the upswing, and the relatively obscure but technically excellent Opera Browser (*www.opera.com*) from Norway is being built into more Web-enabled cellular phones and other non-PC Web access devices every year, and is slowly but steadily gaining market share on PC desktops, especially in Europe. (See Figure 8–1.)

The only true defense against shifts in browser technology is to make sure (a) your site follows display standards laid down by the World Wide Web Consortium (aka W3C), the international group that determines technical specifications for the World Wide Web and (b) that it does not favor one browser over another. Some Web designers will tell you this can't be done, and others will try to talk you into making many different versions of your site, and setting up your servers so they automatically detect which browser each user is running and display the correct version for that browser. A *skilled* Web designer can make an attractive site that works with

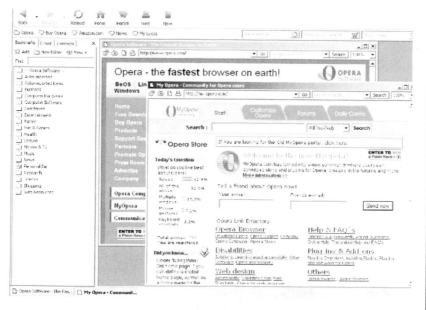

■ **Figure 8–1   Opera Browser offers many features that MSIE lacks, including the ability to stop popup ads and keep animated banners from blinking.**

Users Can and Will Destroy Your Site's Layout

As I write this, I am using the (Open Source) Mozilla 0.9.8 Web browser running on Linux. One of the great features of the Mozilla browser is its ability to "zoom" text. I am old enough that I do not want to tell you how old I am, and I wear bifocals and do most of my work on a laptop with a 14" screen, so I use this feature often.

You can make a site that looks wonderful with the font and font size you or your designer chose, but what happens when I suddenly decide to make all your text a lot bigger than you meant it to be? I can do this with a simple click, and so can any other person using a browser that has a "text zoom" feature.

I talked about the difference between designing for the Web and designing for print publication back in Chapter 2, but a little reminder here that Web designers must be willing to give up the total layout control they would have on paper can't hurt. You can't make two columns on a Web site bottom out evenly the way you can on paper. Don't even

try. If you get it to look right in MSIE on a Mac, it's going to look different in MSIE on a Windows computer anyway, and even if you use browser and operating system detection, and make enough site versions to accommodate every browser you've ever heard of, that still won't take care of the fact that some users have 14" screens and run their browser windows 800 pixels wide, while others have 22" screens and run their browser windows 1400 pixels wide.

Aside from the differences between browsers and operating systems on desktop and laptop computers, there is also the fact that more and more people are accessing the Internet through PDAs, cellular phones, "webtop boxes" mounted on their TVs, and other devices that don't have the same screen characteristics and browser capabilities as full-blown computers.

Simple sites almost always adjust to browser and monitor differences more easily than complex ones, and complex sites almost always display poorly (if at all) on non-PC devices. Never forget this.

almost any browser. It may not have as many baubles and bangles as one designed to look its best with one particular browser and operating system combination, but you are not putting up a Web site to prove that you (or your site designer) know how to use all kinds of cool technologies. You are making it to attract a targeted group of readers or potential customers, and this means your aim is to present information as clearly and simply as you can for many different browser systems.

The Curse of the Obsolete Browser

MSIE versions 5.5 and up, and Netscape 6.0 versions and up, both do a good job of displaying pages that are written in accordance with current _W3C.org_ specifications. But earlier browser versions do not suddenly disappear just because new ones come out. There are businesses and government agencies that still use Windows 98, even Windows 95, and cannot upgrade to the latest browsers. There are also people who are satisfied with their current software installations—the ones they got working "just right" in 1999 and haven't changed since—and are not going to change until a major hardware failure forces them to buy a new computer.

Table 8–1 is an excerpt from the actual browser statistics for a low-volume transportation industry Web site from March, 2002. At the time, the latest MSIE was version 6.0, and the latest Netscape was version 6.21.

Note that the latest browser versions are in the minority. This list includes only browsers and versions that hit this site more than 100 times. 79 users viewed the site on Macs using MSIE 5.01, and hundreds more viewed it on browsers ranging all the way back to Netscape 3, and 31 used text-only browsers that haven't been updated significantly since the mid-90s.

One thing in the above table that shouldn't be taken seriously is the fact that AvantGo (_www.avantgo.com_) is in the number one position. AvantGo is a service, not a browser, and once AvantGo adds a site to its list, its automated crawlers tend to hit it frequently, looking for updates. AvantGo recreates each site that it crawls in a simpler format than appears on a regular monitor screen, and that simplified site is what users of the service see on their PDAs, cellular phones, and other small-screen devices. While the owner of this site is probably happy that AvantGo is showing it to clients,

Table 8–1 An Actual Web Site Log

```
#reqs: browser
  441: Mozilla/3.0 (compatible; AvantGo 3.2)
  362: Mozilla/4.0 (compatible; MSIE 5.01; Windows NT 5.0)
  338: Mozilla/4.0 (compatible; MSIE 6.0; Windows NT 5.1; Q312461)
  304: Mozilla/5.0 (X11; U; Linux i686; en-US; rv:0.9.4)
Gecko/20011126 Netscape6/6.2.1
  301: sitecheck.internetseer.com (For more info see:
http://sitecheck.internetseer.com)
  266: Mozilla/4.0 (compatible; MSIE 6.0; Windows NT 5.0; Q312461)
  240: Mozilla/4.0 (compatible; MSIE 6.0; Windows NT 5.0)
  232: LinksManager.com (http://linksmanager.com/linkchecker.html)
  213: Mozilla/4.0 (compatible; MSIE 5.5; Windows NT 5.0)
  180: Mozilla/3.0 (Slurp/si; slurp@inktomi.com;
http://www.inktomi.com/slurp.html)
  180: Mozilla/4.0 (compatible; MSIE 5.5; Windows NT 5.0; T312461)
  166: Mozilla/4.0 (compatible; MSIE 5.0; Windows 98; DigExt)
  158: Mozilla/4.0 (compatible; MSIE 5.5; Windows 98)
  153: Mozilla/4.0 (compatible; MSIE 6.0; Windows NT 5.1)
  151: Googlebot/2.1 (+http://www.googlebot.com/bot.html)
  141: Mozilla/4.0 (compatible; MSIE 6.0; Windows 98; Q312461)
  141: Mozilla/4.76 [en] (X11; U; Linux 2.2.16-22 i686)
  116: Mozilla/4.0 (compatible; MSIE 5.5; Windows NT 4.0)
  115: Mozilla/4.0 (compatible; MSIE 6.0; Windows 98)
  106: Mozilla/4.0 (compatible; MSIE 5.5; Windows NT 5.0) Fetch API
Request
  104: Mozilla/4.0 (compatible; MSIE 6.0; Windows NT 5.1; Q312461;
MSIECrawler)
  100: Mozilla/4.0 (compatible; MSIE 5.5; Windows 98; Win 9x 4.90)
```

chances are the number of AvantGo users who actually looked at it was much smaller than the 441 displayed in the site statistics.

Interpreting Site Statistics

Site statistics can be fascinating. You should check yours regularly, and read them with a discerning eye. The stat table above told us that not only AvantGo, but also Inktomi, Internetseer, and Google spiders check this site frequently. This means it is probably indexed correctly in most major search engines. There is a separate log provided by most shared hosting services, and that you can produce yourself with any one of a number of free Open Source programs if you run your own servers, that can tell you which URLs sent visitors to yours. This log will help you determine how effective your efforts at getting good search engine listings have been.

You may also find that sites you don't even know about have linked to you, and if you are running banner ad campaigns, the referral log can help you tell how well they're working.

You can also tell how many people have looked at *each page* on your site. If you are displaying products, this is a good gauge of interest in your wares, and a check of the number of sales versus the number of pageviews for each product can tell you what percentage of shoppers who look at each item actually buy it. If you have a few products that consistently draw many lookers, but very few buyers, you need to ask questions. Is the price too high? Is the product illustration unappealing? Is this item often out of stock? Web site statistics cannot answer these questions, but they can certainly help you figure out what questions to ask.

An Endless Learning Process

It doesn't matter whether you are a home-based entrepreneur or a Global 1000 corporate executive, and it doesn't matter whether you are getting ready to launch your first Web site or have been working online for 10 years. You still have a lot to learn about using the Internet as a business tool. We all do.

The commercially-available Internet has been around only since 1994, and widespread use didn't start until 1997 or so. During this short time, advances in the Internet itself and in the computer and software we use to connect to it have been startling. Now we seem to have hit a bit of a plateau, during which some of the original "Golly! Gee whiz!" technologies are maturing and having the bugs whacked out of them. We have had some time to see what works and what doesn't, and more importantly, to see what Internet users want and what they don't want.

Remember "push" technology? We were all going to send endless streams of content to signed-up users' desktops at our convenience, and they were going to access what we sent them whenever they wanted, instantly, without waiting for each page to download. Nothing came of this idea because hardly any Internet users signed up for it. The only "push" technology that has stayed with us is email, and it is being misused so badly as a promotional medium right now that legitimate businesses need to be extra-careful how they use it so that they don't get lumped in with the spam artists who fill our email inboxes with pitches for everything from

Keeping Your Site Up to Date

When you saw this subtitle, your first thought was probably about technology. Groovy new Web tricks seem to come out almost every week. But I am not talking about technology here. Remember all those people with old browsers? They can't use the new technology anyway. Let others pioneer the leading edge. You can always jump on the latest whatever after it's had a few years not only to prove itself and get the kinks worked out, but also to spread widely enough that most of your readers or customers are familiar with it and, if some sort of program on their computer is needed to make use of it, they already have it installed.

What you need to worry about is keeping the information on your site up to date. If Ezra K. Gillicoody leaves the company, his contact information should be removed from your site immediately. When your office in Jakarta gets a new fax number, your site should list the new one right away. A Web site with obsolete information on it reflects badly on your company, and it is a lot easier, faster, and cheaper to change information on a Web site than to change letterheads or business cards.

Prices are critical. In some countries, advertising a price lower than your actual selling price is illegal. Legality aside, customers tend to get irritated when you call or email them and say, "Oh, the price on the Web site is wrong. It's supposed to be $384 higher than that."

This is not a hypothetical situation. It happened to me with a purchase from one of the world's largest computer vendors several years ago. I immediately canceled the order (for a midrange laptop) and swore to myself that I would never deal with that company again. Wouldn't you have done the same? And don't you think this is what plenty of your customers will do to you if you publish a price on your Web site, then tell them it was too low?

There is no legitimate excuse for an incorrect price on a Web site. You can't claim, "The price change came after we sent it to the printer," as can legitimately happen with paper catalogs and fliers. You must make sure that every bit of information on your site is current at every single moment.

Operating a profitable Web site is an ongoing process, not a one-time project. It is not something you "do this week," then move on. It is a long-term commitment. I have watched many sites start with big plans and high hopes only to slowly go downhill once the people who put them up realize that they need to keep them up not just this week and next week, but next year and the year after that.

When most people talk about "futureproofing" a Web site, they are talking about technology. But real futureproofing is a matter of attitude; it is knowing all the way down into your bones that instead of starting your Web site off with a big splash, you should begin humbly, not bite off more than you can chew, and gradually improve over the years as you gain experience.

multilevel marketing scams to "free porn" offers that, somehow, never turn out to be free.

Streaming video was going to be huge, but turned out to be so expensive to produce and deliver compared to what advertisers were prepared to pay to sponsor it that some of the major news Web sites have decided to charge subscription fees to those who want to watch their video clips online. But at the same time, movie studios have found that placing previews—or "trailers," as they are called—on the Internet is an effective promotional technique. Right now the most popular format for movie trailers is Quicktime, a format developed by Apple, not the Windows Media Player which Microsoft has pushed like mad and now includes in every copy of Windows.

Flash, once considered a "way out there" method of delivering animated content over the Internet, has become a staple of Web advertisers, and is rapidly turning into a medium for online artistic expression by cartoonists and graphics designers. Flash still doesn't belong on your Web site's front page, but it may help you to tell a sales story somewhere on your site if you use it wisely— and sparingly.

Companies that produce movies, music, books, software, and other intellectual property are fighting the basic "information sharing" ethos of the Internet's early years. They will win some of their battles and lose others. Sooner or later they will learn new ways of marketing their products online instead of fighting against digital copying, which isn't going to go away no matter how many laws are made that prohibit it. The movie industry reacted with horror to broadcast television but managed to adjust and survive, and later acted the same way toward videocassette sales—and soon after that toward the video rental business—but in the end moviemakers always seem to come up with a way to profit from every new technology they claim will put them out of business once they stop crying on legislators' shoulders and get down to the business of exploiting that technology for profit.

Microsoft is currently king of the computer desktop, and today AOL Time Warner is the world's largest producer and deliverer of content to computer desktops. Each one would like to move into the other's turf. This battle between behemoths is likely to shape much of the Internet's development over the next few years, but the Internet and computer businesses are evolving so rapidly that it is doubtful that either of these companies will ever totally dominate the Internet and all the devices connected to it. And while Microsoft and AOL Time Warner executives—and executives from Sun Microsystems, Oracle, IBM, and other industry giants—take public potshots at one another, the best thing the rest of us can do is lie low. We should pick the best bits of technology from each player in the field and incorporate them into our own businesses while avoiding lockins with any one company by using as much Open Source software as we can, and building our Web sites and other "core" online activities around open, industry-wide standards.

In the middle of all this turbulence, those of us who use the Internet intelligently as a business tool, instead of treating it as an end in and of itself, have a chance to create little online islands of sanity for our readers and customers. We may not get rich overnight, but that's okay. We will build our profits steadily, rationally, and with minimal risk. We will study the consequences of each online move we make before we make it. We will, in other words, be prudent business people who adhere to the basic tenet, "To earn a profit, you must take in more money than you spend," that has served our predecessors well since the idea of "business" was first invented, long before historical records were kept.

Resources

Here are 12 essential books and Web sites that will help you make an attractive and usable Web site, use email profitably, and generally work with and on the Internet. This list is just a starting place. The Internet itself is changing too fast for any print book to keep up with all the resources on or about it, and that's why the first listing is this book's companion Web site.

1. *BuildProfitsOnline.com*

This is where you can read and contribute corrections, additions, and updates to what you have just read in *The Online Rules of Successful Companies*. You'll see stories about people who are making money on the Internet and how they're doing it, along with other readers' comments about those stories. And if you have an online business success story of your own, this is the place to share it!

2. *Designing Web Usability: The Practice of Simplicity*

By Jakob Nielsen (New Riders Publishing; ISBN: 156205810X; First Edition, December 1999)

Nielsen is the "king" of online usability. If you are a serious Web site builder, you must read this book. You may not want to follow all of Nielsen's advice, but you should know what he says before you start deviating from the rules he lays down for usable site design.

3. *Zeldman.com*

Follow the latest trends in Web design, brought to you by one of the world's most respected online graphics gurus. Use Jeffrey Zeldman's many free tutorials to learn everything from basic HTML to the latest in cascading style sheets, buy Zeldman's excellent book, *Taking Your Talent to the Web*, at *www.zeldman.com/talent/*, hang out with leading and aspiring Web designers at A List Apart. This is an amazing resource for Web designers and those who deal with them.

4. *HTML 4 for the World Wide Web*

By Elizabeth Castro (Peachpit Press; ISBN: 0201354934; Fourth Edition, October 20, 1999)

Castro has been writing practical, well-illustrated HTML authoring manuals almost since the beginning of the World Wide Web. It's best to get the latest edition, although you can't go wrong starting with an older version, since the basics haven't changed all that much. Castro's books are found next to many designers' keyboards, used as references even by people who have years of experience writing HTML and other site-producing code, even though they are really aimed at beginners.

5. *Webmonkey.com*

Webmonkey is a constantly-updated, "check it regularly" Web design resource, with sections for beginners, builders and masters. It's been around for over five years, and over that time it has built up a huge library of code snippets, links, and tutorials that can help you do things like create cool forms and other Javascript and CGI goodies and get them right the first time—even if you've never messed with Javascript before.

6. *Logistics and Supply Chain Management: Strategies for Reducing Cost and Improving Service*

By Martin Christopher (Prentice Hall PTR; ISBN 0273630490; Second Edition, 1998)

This one is listed here specifically for ecommerce hopefuls who need help setting up everything that goes *behind* their Web sites, an area that many online businesses have forgotten can make or break them—and that has broken more than one.

7. *Webpagesthatsuck.com*

This site has been around for a long, long time. You don't want it to link to yours. Vincent Flanders, who runs it, has made a career out of pointing to bad Web sites and showing people how not to make one. He's written two books (that you can buy through his site), he gives speeches, he does consulting. As long as people and businesses keep on making bad Web sites, Flanders will make a living. Sadly, it looks like he's going to have plenty of material to keep going for the rest of his life.

8. *Permission-Based E-Mail Marketing That Works!*

By Kim MacPherson (Dearborn Trade; ISBN: 0793142954; May 2001)

Once you get beyond the exclamation point in the title and some of the "Isn't the Internet wonderful!" copy, what you have here is one of the few books ever written that tells you how to use email as a practical marketing and customer relations device, in great detail, including sample cost figures for various types of campaigns. (Note that this is not a spammer's manual. Spam is bad. We don't like spam around here.)

9. *Clickz.net*

It's a site for, by, and about online marketers, full of marketing tips and tricks for both large and small businesses, with an emphasis on rah-rah direct sales tactics.

10. *The Online Copywriter's Handbook: Everything You Need to Know to Write Online Copy That Sells*

By Robert W. Bly (McGraw Hill - NTC; ISBN: 0658021141; Second Edition, February 20, 2002)

This is the best guide to writing online advertising copy out there right now. Bly was already justifiably famous for *The Copywriter's Handbook*, a classic in the "how to write powerful ad copy" field that came out in 1984, well before the Internet was a sales medium—or even open to the public. Don't forget: You can make a lovely site with a great navigation scheme, but in the end it's your words that get them to buy the product.

11. *IAB.net*

The Interactive Advertising Bureau (IAB) calls itself, "The first global not-for-profit association devoted exclusively to maximizing the use and effectiveness of advertising on the Internet," and that's exactly what it is. Keep an eye on this site for the latest trends in online advertising. It's also the place to find out about standard banner ad sizes and presentation methods. Whether you're on the buying or selling end of the online advertising business, IAB is an essential resource.

12. *Sitecritique.net*

Think of this site as peer review for your site, as well as a valuable look at what others are doing, categorized by type of business, and how they were rated by other Web site owners. If you are getting ready to make your first Web site (or to redesign one you already have) a look through _Sitecritique.net_ can save you time and money. Free registration is required for some site features, and "professional" critiques are available for a small additional fee. Either way, using _Sitecritique.net_ is lots cheaper than paying a marketing research company to run focus groups, and both the peer review feature and professional reviews here seem to be right on target.

Index

A

A List Apart, 35-37, 175
ActiveX, 152
Advertising
  banner, 79, 142
  banner exchange, 143
  business of selling, 12
  cross-fertilization, 149
  delivery vehicle, 94
  economic realities, 84-86
  online, 2, 141-42
  offline, 142, 144
  popup, 165
  revenue, 12
  sales projections, 91
  tech-oriented, 24
  text ads online, 141-42
  Web site as, 3
AllTheWeb, 131
AltVista, 131
AOL, 121, 165, 172
AOLsearch, 131
Amazon.com, 10
Andover News Network, 80-81
Apache, 55, 163-64
Apple, 172
Ask Jeeves, 131
AvantGo, 168

B

Bandwidth, 156
Bates, Jeff, 80-82
Big Blue Room, 68
Boolean, 134-35
Brochureware, 11
Browsers, 74, 164-69
  AvantGo, 168
  crashing, 18-19

display differences, 166-67
industry standards, 164-65
Internet Explorer, 25, 164,167
Mozilla, 165-66
Netscape, 25, 165-67
obsolete, 167
Opera, 25, 165
statistics, 168-69
window sizes, 25-27
BSD, 163
BuildProfitsOnline.com, 24-25, 175
Business, stick to, 77

C

Cascading Style Sheets (CSS), 28
Catalog, 2-3
CEO, 36
  picture of, 41
CGI, 29
Chaney, Michael, 71-72
Chat, 103, 118-20
  AOL, 121
  addiction, 122-23
  as internal tool, 121-23
  customer service, 119-20
  etiquette, 124-27
  ICQ, 121
  IRC, 121-23
  Jabber, 122
  teenage, 125
  Yahoo!, 121
Chiu, Alex, 6
Client Server NEWS, 111
CmdrTaco, 80
C|Net 88, 93
CNN, 95
CPM, 85
Community
  online, 8-10

OSDN produces award-winning sites that deliver the best content to a tightly knit, collaborative, tech savvy audience who influence and make critical purchasing decisions for their companies.

A Network of Web Sites.

Millions of Influential High-tech Professionals.

Geocrawler
The Knowledge Archive

http://osdn.com

8 reasons why you should read the Financial Times for 4 weeks RISK-FREE!

To help you stay current with significant
developments in the world economy ...
and to assist you to make informed business
decisions — the Financial Times brings you:

❶ Fast, meaningful overviews of international affairs ... plus daily
briefings on major world news.

❷ Perceptive coverage of economic, business, financial and political
developments with special focus on emerging markets.

❸ More international business news than any other publication.

❹ Sophisticated financial analysis and commentary on world market
activity plus stock quotes from over 30 countries.

❺ Reports on international companies and a section on global investing.

❻ Specialized pages on management, marketing, advertising and
technological innovations from all parts of the world.

❼ Highly valued single-topic special reports (over 200 annually)
on countries, industries, investment opportunities, technology and more.

❽ The Saturday Weekend FT section — a globetrotter's guide to
leisure-time activities around the world: the arts, fine dining, travel,
sports and more.

FT FINANCIAL TIMES
World business newspaper

The *Financial Times* delivers
a world of business news.

Use the Risk-Free Trial Voucher below!

To stay ahead in today's business world you need to be well-informed on a daily basis. And not just on the national level. You need a news source that closely monitors the entire world of business, and then delivers it in a concise, quick-read format.

With the *Financial Times* you get the major stories from every region of the world. Reports found nowhere else. You get business, management, politics, economics, technology and more.

Now you can try the *Financial Times* for 4 weeks, absolutely risk free. And better yet, if you wish to continue receiving the *Financial Times* you'll get great savings off the regular subscription rate. Just use the voucher below.

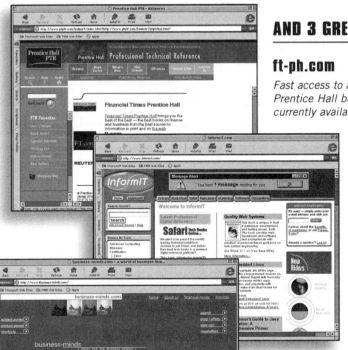